The Digital Crystal Ball

*Your Personal Electronic Astrology,
Tarot, Numerology, and I Ching Advisor*

Guy D. Smith

LIGHTSPEED PUBLISHING

© 1996 Guy D. Smith

Published by LightSpeed Publishing, Inc.
PO Box 1120
Glen Ellen, California 95442-1120
http://www.lsp.com/people/calamar

Publishers: Scott Calamar & Joel Fugazzotto
Development & Editing: Scott Calamar
Cover Design: Pat and Michael Rogondino
Design and Production: Michele Cuneo

LightSpeed Publishing is distributed to bookstores and book wholesalers in the
United States and Canada by Publishers Group West, PO Box 8843, Emeryville,
California, 94662, 1-800-788-3123 (510-658-3453 in California).

Illustrations from the Rider-Waite Tarot Deck® reproduced by permission of U.S. Games
Systems, Inc., Stamford, CT 06902 USA. Copyright © 1971 by U.S. Games Systems, Inc.
Further reproduction prohibited. The Rider-Waite Tarot Deck® is a registered trademark
of U.S. Games System, Inc.

All programs distributed with this book are done so with the permission of their authors or
copyright holders. We thank them for their cooperation.

All terms mentioned in this book that are known to be registered trademarks, trademarks,
or service marks have been appropriately capitalized. All product names mentioned in this
book are trademarks, registered trademarks, or service marks of their respective owners.

While every precaution has been taken in the preparation of this book, neither the author
nor LightSpeed Publishing shall have any liability to any person or entity with respect to
any loss or damage caused, or alleged to be caused, directly or indirectly by the instructions
contained in this book or by the computer software products included in this package.

Printed in the United States of America
First printing, 1996
ISBN 1-887132-01-5

Dedication

To my mother,
Mary Terentiak Smith
(1931-1992)

Acknowledgments

Guy D. Smith would like to thank Nancy Connally for all her assistance with the graphic captures and her willingness to allow me to totally mess up her Windows desktop configuration in the process....my father, Jack D. Smith, for always being such an unusual bird, and establishing similar (but different) sorts of peculiar interests and proclivities in me at an early age....Alice Higgins for all her moral support during the development of the book (and all the missed lunches)....all the software developers and distributors who generously contributed their time and efforts to make sure we had the best divination software and information included in the book...and especially Scott Calamar of LightSpeed for taking a chance on an unproven entity, and having the faith (and patience) to help me see it through to the end - thanks, Scott.

The publishers are greatly indebted to the many software authors and distributors for kindly allowing us to distribute their first-class programs. Many took their valuable time to create special versions or worked with us in other ways. Thanks to:

Guy Damian-Knight and Annie Fisher of Tao Management for Decision Track

Harold Feist of oTherlobe for Prime

Christiaan Freeling and Ed van Zon of Solar Software for I Ching Connexion

Katie Intrieri and Jeff Manning of Virtual Media Works for Virtual Tarot

Greg Katsoulis for Fortune Teller

Rustle Laidman for Rosarium

David Lartique for 8-Ball for Windows

Larry Malakoff of Widening Horizons for Personal Numerology and Intimacy

Elena Mildenberger of LifeStyle Software Group and Nathan Tennies for Visions

Christopher J. Noyes for ASTRO for Windows

Paul O'Brien of Synchronicity Software for Synchronicity

Ed Perrone for AstroEphemeris

Neil Shulman for Mac Predictions

Anthony Vazquez for Tarot Reader

We appreciate the help of John McMahon for supplying the Tarot card images from his web site and we also want to say thanks to Myra Anderson for her wonderfully illustrated pictures.

Also, many thanks to Michael and Pat Rogondino for a beautiful cover and the kindness to nurture a fledgling publisher, and to Michele Cuneo, for another tastefully beautiful design and desktop publishing job.

We would also like to offer thanks to Joel and Brenda Fugazzotto for their support and encouragement throughout this exciting venture.

And finally, thanks to author Guy Smith who threw himself into this project and made the process as extraordinary as the forces this book is about.

About The Author

Guy D. Smith is a video and multimedia writer, designer, and producer/director living in Dallas, Texas. He was most recently seen heading south towards Austin in search of the wisdom of the ancients, a stained and tattered copy of the Tao Te Ching and a Powerbook tucked under his arm. *The Digital Crystal Ball* is his first book.

Table of Contents

PART ONE

Welcome to the Digital Crystal Ball

*There are more things in heaven and earth,
Horatio, than are dreamt of in your philosophy*

- William Shakespeare, Hamlet, Act 1, Scene 5

If you don't know the difference between Ram Dass and ROM DOS, an emphemeris from an epiphany, or a Yarrow stick from a popsicle stick, then you've come to the right place...

You're holding this book for a reason. You've selected it for a reason. ☯ There are no accidents, you know.

Maybe you have a subconscious urge to dabble in divination on your computer. ☯ Or maybe you're simply curious about the intricacies of Astrology, the esoteric imagery of the Tarot, the ancient wisdom of the I Ching, or the science of Numerology.

In any case, you've got the urge to stretch your psychic muscles a bit - to see just what the stars, cards, hexagrams, and numbers might hold in store for you and your friends.

Or, maybe - just maybe - you didn't select the book at all, but rather this book selected you...Maybe there's a message out there - seeking you - and it's decided to reach you through your computer...

The Digital Crystal Ball is all about using your computer for "divination." We've gathered some of the best metaphysical software available and have put it on the CD-ROM included with the book.

First, we'll introduce you to divination - specifically, divination by computer. Then we'll help you get your system booted up, and finally - we'll look at the divination methodologies, with some history and details about each.

In each specific divination section -

● The Online Astrologer,

● The Magic of the Tarot: Pick a Card, Any Card,

● I Ching: The Book of Changes and Your Destiny, and

● By the Numbers: Numerology Tells All,

there's an easy to follow, step-by-step guide to loading, opening, and using each of the key divination programs found on the CD-ROM...easy even for those of you who use your computer only to play games - or as just a glorified (albeit colorful) typewriter.

We've also included a section in the back of the book that is a resource guide to where you can get additional information about divination (including online services such as America Online, Compuserve, etc.). We've listed some sources for additional divination software, some locations to check out on the Internet, and finally, a bibliography that lists other good resource texts that you can obtain to learn more about the fascinating history, lore, and practice of divination.

We've tried to make navigating around the CD-ROM a breeze, but if you're new to computers, we suggest you spend a few minutes with the section entitled "Your Journey Begins: Boot up the Computer and See the Light" before venturing onto the CD-ROM itself. There we get you started off on the right foot, discussing the basics you need to know about starting up your computer and accessing the programs on the CD-ROM.

So...kick off those wingtips and slip on your Birkenstocks, brew up a nice big pot of herbal tea, dim the lights, breathe deeply (a touch of incense, perhaps?), put a little Kitaro on the CD player, and sit back and read over the next couple of chapters first, before you load that CD-ROM...

Trust me, you'll thank yourself later for doing so. And who knows? It might even improve your Karma and save you from living through one incarnation as a computer-illiterate toad. (If you think computers are big now, just wait until your next life!)

Computer Users Quickstart: Divining, er, Diving Right In

So - brave soul - you're ready to just "dive in" into the programs, huh? That's great, if you're somewhat familiar with computer operation.

Perhaps you may already know some portion (or a good deal) of the computer basics and navigation skills we'll cover in the book. If so, you may want to go ahead and just get busy poking around. The following information should be enough to get you started:

The book gives in-depth information about operating the key programs for the following four divination methods:

  Astrology (IBM - *Astro for Windows*, Mac - *Visions Demo*)

  Tarot (*Virtual Tarot Demo* for both IBM and Mac)

● The I Ching (*Synchronicity Demo* for both IBM and Mac)

● Numerology (IBM - *Personal Numerologist* and *Intimacy*, Mac - *Prime Demo*).

Macintosh: If your CD-ROM player is properly connected and the driver software is properly installed, an icon representing the *Digital Crystal Ball* CD-ROM should appear on your Finder desktop. Inside you will find folders (and icons) for the programs mentioned above. Be sure to open the file called "Read Me First!" It will have information not included in the book concerning changes, errata, etc.

IBM: As with the Macintosh, assuming your CD-ROM player is properly connected and your driver software is properly installed, you should be able to locate the CD-ROM as drive "D" via either DOS or Windows. (If your CD-ROM is not drive "D" see Chapter 2.) The name of the directory on the CD-ROM containing all the programs will be called DCBALL. Inside it, look for a file called "DCBINFO.TXT"; it will contain information concerning changes, errata, etc. not included in the book. The other directories - ASTROLGY, ICHING, NUMRLGY, and TAROT - are where your programs for each of the four divination techniques are located.

For both IBM and Macintosh you will find an additional folder or directory ("Goodies" for the Macintosh and "GOODIES" for the IBM) which contains extra divination programs and utilities for you to explore - some serious and some just for fun. Their operation is not discussed in the book per se, but where needed, on-screen help or manuals are generally available to assist you.

Remember that the book offers some real gold nuggets of information for you about the history and lore of each of the divination techniques (and might even provide you with a little "divine intervention" should you have a problem with the software). Have a great time exploring!

1

Digital Divination: Gazing into the Crystal Screen

Men are probably nearer the central truth in their superstitions than in their science.

- Henry David Thoreau

Sensitivity and Silicon - A Brief Look at Divination

A book about metaphysical software almost sounds oxymoronic, doesn't it? Using the latest computer hardware to practice divination techniques as old as the history of man has an odd feel somehow - a juxtaposition of spirituality and technology, human intuitiveness and silicon-based logic, and the contrast of the "yes/no" binary process of the computer with the multipolar - almost organic - process of divining the future.

An odd concept perhaps, but certainly a compelling one, as well.

In the last several years, it seems that there has been a quiet, but growing, revival of interest among many individuals - from all walks of life - in things spiritual and metaphysical.

If there is a common thread in the New Age worldview, it is that - in spite of how good we *should* have it here in the waning hours of the late Twentieth century - something seems to be amiss. We don't seem to have the answers to solve the problems our advancing "civilization" creates in the name of progress. We've lost touch with something and are seeking desperately to get the ill-defined and elusive "it" back.

The tired, time-honored formulas and answers that worked so well for our parents and their parents before them no longer seem to apply to us. A casual perusal of the popular media reveals evidence of a malaise for which no one -

neither government, nor the churches, nor the corporations which so pervade our daily lives - seems to be able to provide the answers.

Consider the following - we have technology which gives us instantaneous access to events occurring anywhere in the world in a matter of seconds, we have computers which can produce imagery which blurs and often erases the boundaries between fantasy and reality, and space travel has become such a cliché that a Space Shuttle launch barely makes the evening news anymore.

Not bad progress for a species who, not that long ago, had to gain its daily bread by climbing down from trees and scooting across the savannah to fight off its hyena neighbors for carrion at the local watering hole.

But, for some reason, instead of our technological progress making us happier and more independent, it seems to have only plagued us with more questions and spiritual challenges. Paradoxically, living has gotten easier - and harder - at the same time

Materially, we are better off now than we've ever been in the history of the species. The marvels of virtual reality perch on our doorsteps (and desktops) and yet - spiritually and psychically - it appears that we're virtually bankrupt - and we're not sure why.

Many feel that the answers might lie in the wisdom of the traditions of our ancient ancestors.

The Rhythms and Wisdom of the Ancients

In the ancient past, humans integrated the activities of their lives into the rhythms and patterns of their environment. Our lives were simpler, based on the cycles of nature...the turn of the seasons...the rising and setting of the sun, the moon and the stars...the natural cycle of birth, growth, and - ultimately - death and eventual reintegration back into the larger flow of life.

People viewed their lives holistically - as part of a larger mechanism of nature which provided them with all they needed - shelter, food, and clothing. And, if listened to carefully, with the proper reverence, the right tools, and tuned sensitivities - nature could and would provide guidance and answers to the plaguing questions of life. Hence, the process of divination became as critical a tool for human survival as the use of an axe, a spear - or even fire.

In today's world we seem to spend a great deal of energy fighting against these basic rhythms of life. We live our lives largely "anti-holistically." Our entire reason for living seems to be to subdue the powers of nature and its natural rhythms and cycles, and to instill our own artificial system of reality - insisting on "improving" on it somehow.

In today's modern world, our careers generally comes first, our family second (Remember them? That loose group of equally busy individuals who live in your house?), and the remaining time is allocated to what we loosely describe as "living" - a regimen of exercise, education, reproducing, eating, vacations, communicating, being entertained, etc., etc., until one day we just sort of - ready or not - check out.

Don't you just hate it when that happens?

The Role of Divination in Society

Whether or not a dog or an aardvark or an amoeba has the cognitive powers necessary to contemplate life's meaning - why it's here, and where it's going after its last meal - is most definitely beyond the scope of this book. But it's pretty much a truism that Mankind is probably singular amongst living creatures in its never-ending search to derive meaning for his existence.

The history of divination is a history of Mankind's searching for meaning and is as old as humanity itself.

It's probably when humans evolved from being solitary hunter/gatherers and began to grow their food and to domesticate livestock in a communal society that the knowledge of the intricacies of natural cycles became an important issue, and a critical survival skill. It became critical to understand - and predict with some accuracy - when the rainy season was coming, when to plant and when to harvest. It was also pretty awe-inspiring to be able to predict a solar eclipse or the odd meteorite shower...it got a lot of credibility brownie points in ancient society.

The important knowledge of natural cycles was generally assigned to individuals or groups - medicine men, shaman, priests and priestesses - who had the requisite knowledge and skills to deal with the 'powers of nature.' These people, through apprenticeships and/or demonstrated spiritual sensitivities, were cloaked with the responsibility of interpreting events, predicting the future, and advising the leaders of the tribe on issues involving, not only the weather, but the welfare of the society at large, and the health and well-being of its individual members.

The tools you will be using in this book (the I Ching, the Tarot, Numerology, and Astrology) are rich in that same ancient tradition…steeped in the histories, mythologies, superstitions and religions of our world and its peoples.

By participating in the process of divination using one or all of these tools on your computer, you are not simply delving into an entertaining pastime. Rather, you are also a link in an unbroken chain that extends back to the first person who stared heavenward and contemplated his or her position in the cosmos.

The Computer and Divination, or Do Bits and Bytes have a Buddha Nature?

Whether or not there is an inherent metaphysical "something" missing in a computerized Celtic Cross card spread or an I Ching hexagram casting is a question of some controversy. It doesn't take a Ph.D. to recognize that there are no coins, cards, or yarrow sticks included with the book - just a CD-ROM with a suite of programs.

Can divination by computer really be considered legitimate? Is an inanimate object - such as a computer - really as good as a skilled Tarot reader or a knowledgeable astrologer in providing insight, or is it not just simply a fancy random number generator? Where's the "touch" in the process of divination by computer?

Maybe the larger question here is - what is the role of "tools" in the divination process?

Basically, divination has always been done by one of two methods - either through direct contact with the "spirit world" by individuals in an induced trance state, or - more commonly - through the observation of some event, such as the shape of a cloud, the appearance of a totem animal, or the deliberate throwing of bones, tossing of coins, spread of cards, etc.

All the divination methods dealt within this book - Astrology, Tarot, I Ching and Numerology - fall into the latter category. We're not doing the direct spirit connect thing here.

(If you do go into a trance as a result of these programs, I suggest you get up and fix yourself a nice hot cup of java - maybe check to see if your belt's on too tight.)

Here's where some may have a difference of opinion with me - in many respects the computer is no more (or less) a direct divination tool than an inanimate deck of cards, a handful of dry yarrow sticks, or an ancient book of Chinese wisdom (I hesitate to make a comparison between the steaming entrails of a goat and my PowerMac - but I think you get the point.) The issue is one more of process or significance of ritual, than of physical tools.

In the divination processes we're using, the computer is doing two main things. First, it is doing what computers do best - number crunching and cross-linking databases.

This is evidenced in the derivation of ephemeris information in the astrology programs, the numerical 'reduction' and delineation processes in the numerology programs, and the interpretive readings of both the Tarot and I Ching (in both

10

cases, the computer consults large textual databases to provide a reading for a particular card in a particular position in the Celtic Cross card spread, or finds and delivers the meaning of a particular changing line of an I Ching hexagram).

Secondly - and perhaps more importantly - the computer (and your interaction with it) provides the very important function of giving you a focus point for the process of divination. The very process of sitting down and starting a program is a deliberate act causing you to mentally shift gears - putting you in a more receptive, intuitive mood.

If you know anyone (yourself perhaps?) who is a heavy computer user, you know that sometimes it's hard to figure out where the computer stops and the person begins, or vice versa. The computer and the user seem to be "one" - a "flow" exists between the two entities - man (or woman) and machine. Sometimes, the symbiosis can be pretty scary. My point being that any argument that says a computer isn't as engaging or effective, from a divinatory standpoint, as a deck of cards or a bunch of sticks, is simply off the mark.

While we don't suggest that you do the Vulcan Mindmeld with your Mac or your Compaq, we do suggest that - for any of the divination processes to have usefulness to you - you should approach them with a certain degree of solemnity and focus.

As you use the Synchronicity program, for example, you'll note that the first part of the program is specifically designed to encourage you to calm down and to focus on the issue you are inquiring about - assuming a meditative or contemplative state, if you will. This is done through both visual and auditory cues (love those frogs). I encourage you to stretch your imagination a little and participate in the "texture" that is being provided by the multimedia aspects of the program. Note that all the imagery - the hut and chair, the flickering candle, the table, the stream, the noises of the night - all tie together in a cohesive whole. A bit of theater is going on here - let your hair down and get involved. Engage with the process; after all, that *is* why you bought this, isn't it? To *engage* with the divination process?

Getting Personal - Engaging your Energies with the Keyboard

The actual *mechanics* of the process of divination - casting the I Ching hexagrams and laying out the card spreads of the Tarot - are done in a highly participative manner by you (sometimes referred to as the "querent") through your interaction with the computer keyboard and mouse. While you don't *actually* shuffle cards or toss coins or go through a yarrow stick manipulation process (trust me, you don't want to, either), you *are* very engaged in the process of selection and differentiation. Built into the programs are sophisticated programming do-dads called **algorithms** which simulate the processes of shuffling and spreading the cards, tossing the coins, etc.

The advantage to you is that it all occurs automatically, and a nice feature is that you can't lose the coins or cards, nor spill coffee across the card spread. Now coffee across your keyboard is another issue altogether...

In contrast, Numerology and Astrology are more 'derivative' divination methodologies, depending less upon the interaction of you and the computer at the moment, and more upon past 'external' events (i.e., the position of heavenly bodies or your parents' choices of names when you were born). An argument could be made that it is in these two methods (given the number crunching involved) that using a computer is more legitimate and apropos.

One thing that a computer *cannot* provide you with is the intuitive insights that a sensitive, experienced Tarot reader or I Ching caster can provide. Oft times the messages and symbology of readings seem vague - a strange card or an odd hexagram pops up in a seemingly inappropriate manner or location. Sometimes a message is there, but you just don't see it. A human intermediary, experienced in interpretation, can take information about the reading and through his or her knowledge about your situation and intuition, provide you with possibly useful information - focused on your life's situation.

One thing to keep in mind regarding all divination methodologies is that they are not static, but historically speaking, are evolving beasts. The rituals and tools used today for casting the I Ching, and those used in 1000 BC, are quite different (and the turtles are thankful for it). The Tarot deck used in 1480 in Italy is different than that found in the local bookstore. A hundred years from now - they'll both be different than today (more like what you'll find on the CD-ROM, I would venture to guess).

Arguing which is best - casting the I Ching with yarrow sticks, tortoise shells, coins or a computer program - is akin to asking which is best - a book, a play at a theater, or a videotape. Purists and aficionados aside - the inherent purpose of the book, play and video is similar - to tell a story or to 'receive' one. Of course the experience is different in each - but the message is largely the same. The inherent purpose of the divination process - by cards, coins, or computer - is equally simple. You perform a divination process to receive insightful messages and guidance from time-honored divination tools - not to perform a rote ritual in a monkey-see, monkey-do manner.

A larger, more encompassing world view - an ancient one actually - poses that there is an "interconnectedness" between all things - every atom is intimately and profoundly connected to all the others in the universe. In this view, there is little difference between cards, yarrow sticks, and computers...insight is as likely to come from "the smile of a dog" as from contemplation of a religious tome.

Divination...and Common Sense

While divination can be useful in providing insight into alternatives in your life and can enrich you spiritually, it's important to remember that you - ultimately - are responsible for all aspects of your life. Any actions taken in response to a reading received through divination are your responsibility.

First and foremost, divination should be thought of as just another useful tool in your life - another blade in your cognitive Swiss Army knife, so to speak.

My personal belief is that the process of divination is most useful in providing focus and opening your mind to alternative viewpoints on a problem or issue ("Why haven't I thought of looking at the issue/problem/relationship/etc. from that perspective before?").

Divination can increase your sensitivities to the feelings and predicaments of others...It can enhance your creativity...It can amplify your awareness of the machinations of your own life...but it cannot solve your problems nor replace common sense.

I cannot stress the following advice strongly enough: Just as the use of a computer isn't intended to replace thinking, the use of divination isn't intended to replace common sense. Consult your family, friends, physician, or other professional counselor for advice if you have any serious life issues affecting your health, financial status, relationships, etc.

2

Your Journey Begins: Boot Up Your Computer and See the Light

Faith may be defined briefly as an illogical belief in the occurrence of the improbable.

- H. L. Mencken

In this part of the book, we'll look first at a little introductory information about PCs and CD-ROMs. If you're getting antsy and just want to get started on your computer, go ahead and skip forward to the section entitled "Ladies and Gentlemen - Start your Engines!"

PC Means More than Just "Politically Correct"

Personal Computers, or PCs, are found today in one out of every three households in America, and are rapidly becoming as commonplace as VCRs, projection televisions, fax machines, and cellular telephones.

Manufactured under various names (IBM, Apple, Dell, Toshiba, Compaq, NEC, etc.), what we think of as the "Personal Computer" started out primarily as a tool for business, but very rapidly migrated into the home environment, creating real impact on the way people ran their non-business lives, as well as their businesses.

Personal computers in homes have become entertainment centers, creativity tools for budding artists and writers, research centers for students via online hookups into university and library systems, and windows to the world via the cornucopic variety of services available on the "Information Highway."

From Humble Beginnings....

The first PCs were not what you would think of as things of elegance or beauty. Barely usable in today's terms, they were expensive, slow, had very little memory, no color, no graphics, and...sound?...well, other than the grinding sound of a cassette drive or the 5.25" (and in some cases 8") floppy disk drive, about all you could expect from the first PCs was an occasional obnoxious beep.

Most of the original players in the PC business are gone, having either gone out of business or been gobbled up by growth-hungry competitors. But a few have gone on to become household names - Apple and IBM to mention a couple.

As opposed to what a lot of people think, the term "PC" doesn't have a brand name attached to it...a PC can be *either* an IBM (or compatible) or an Apple Macintosh computer.

A big question is - Why are there two flavors of Personal Computers anyway? How did we end up with both Macintoshes and IBM machines?

Comparing Apples to IBMs

Take a look at the computer you're using. Do you know if it's an IBM compatible or an Macintosh? Chances are if it has a multi-colored Apple emblazoned on the front of it, it's a Macintosh. (Note however, that Apple "clones" are hitting the market, too.)

If it's made by IBM, Tandy, NEC, Compaq, Dell, Toshiba, Hewlett Packard, or a host of other "clone" manufacturers, it's an IBM-PC compatible. Most of you know the difference. A big clue is what "operating system" the computer runs. If it's DOS or Windows, it's an IBM-type. If it has a "Macintosh desktop," it's a Mac. It is getting increasingly difficult to tell the Macintosh operating system from Windows from OS/2, but your first mission is to determine which computer you have.

Arguing about which computer is better is akin to arguing about which car or shoe or brand of underwear is better...to a very large extent, the issue is one of personal taste (and your personal susceptibility to marketing hype).

IBM

Let's face it - as far as computer history and influence goes - the proverbial "IBM-PC" is *the* office and home computer. Millions of IBMs (or clones sometime referred to as "compatibles") are found around the world in locations as unlikely as Buddhist monasteries in Tibet (where they are being used to help document and catalog centuries of Tibetan Buddhist literature) and have become as ubiquitous as the telephone and coffee machine in virtually every office and business in the world.

The computerization of the world has occurred - in large part - to the acceptance of the "IBM machines" and their operating systems called DOS (generally MS-DOS, a product of the Microsoft software company), and Windows (another Microsoft product...any surprise why its owner Bill Gates is a multi-billionaire?).

The MS-DOS operating system was the first IBM operating system and has much built-in utility (despite its archaic text-based interface), and, up until very recently, is still the basis for operating the PC platform; as a matter of fact, until Windows 95, Windows required DOS to be in place in order to operate.

Windows grew out of a need to create an easier, more intuitive way to operate an IBM-PC or clone. Based partially on the success and acceptance of the Macintosh GUI (Graphic User Interface - pronounced "gooey"), Windows was introduced as an 'alternative' to DOS, incorporating the use of a mouse, icons, pulldown menus, windows, etc., to perform the tasks of 'desktop' management (opening files or programs, accessing directories, and so forth). A Windows user can easily navigate back and forth between the two operating systems (Windows and DOS) as necessary. Because some of the programs found on your CD-ROM are Windows and some are DOS, it will be necessary for you to do so - but don't worry. The procedure for doing so is straightforward, and the operations of each program will be explained.

Macintosh

After its introduction in 1984, the Mac rapidly became a counter-cultural alternative into the world of data processing. One of the reasons why the Mac has become so widely accepted (particularly by the 'right-brained' set - artists, illustrators, designers, writers, etc.) is because of its unique user interface. With the introduction of the Mac, a new intuitive paradigm of working with a computer was born - icons, menus, and an interface device called a "mouse" replaced the text-laden DOS system. The name of the computer itself was creatively compelling - the Apple Macintosh (even the name "Apple" harkens to the Garden of Eden and the enlightenment of our species...slightly more than "IBM-PC-XT" did anyway).

Using a Macintosh hasn't changed that much (at least to the end-user) over the 10 years or so since its introduction; the icons, menus, and mouse are still there. But in an effort to incorporate the changing demands of the end-user and the ever-expanding computer industry, the Macintosh operating system has had to grow and "expand" somewhat - but still maintains the intuitive icon and mouse-driven interface.

Once the Mac was introduced, it didn't take long for IBM and Microsoft to get the message. The funny little "bar of soap" mouse , and the "cute little pictures" made sense - at least a lot more intuitive sense than "c:\>" anyway. Soon the IBMers had Microsoft Windows, and the line between the two different camps - IBMers and Macintosh users - suddenly became very thin.

The reality is there's more similarity between the Mac and IBM systems (at least from a user standpoint) than there is difference, and ten years from now (or sooner), they'll likely be virtually indistinguishable...as a Chevy is from a Ford.

The bottom line? Today, for about $2500, you can buy a complete computer package (either a Macintosh or an IBM/compatible) with a CPU, keyboard, and monitor that will deliver photo-realistic color, 3-D animation, stereo sound, with a processor that computes at a speed of 60+ megahertz (for comparison, the original IBM-PC worked at only 8 megahertz)...not to mention a CD-ROM drive and half a gigabyte (500 megabytes) hard drive to go with it....and stereo speakers, to boot! The rest...as they say...is just details.

Who's Computing?

Let's talk a little about the kinds of folks out there who have a computer...you're in here somewhere.

On one end of the spectrum, there are the folks who seem to have been born with a mouse in one hand and a keyboard in the other. These people are fairly easy to recognize because they don't seem to speak in a language the rest of us can understand.

Their idea of a good time on Saturday night is formatting a new box of floppy disks, adding more RAM memory to their motherboard, and cruising the Internet at 28.8 kps talking about "web pages," FTP sites, and virtual locations that have names like "http://alt.com.bevo.edu.net/~zanzibar". If you understand any of what I just said, congratulations - you're a certified geek. Knock yourself out browsing the CD-ROM.

On the other end of the scale is the computer neophyte. People in this category are generally reluctant to even touch a keyboard for fear of permanent damage to either themselves or the computer. You may find these folks wandering around computer stores staring at boxes of software scratching their heads, or reading specs of computer systems trying to make sense of the techno-gobbledygook which is ubiquitous to the computer business. (Paradoxically, they're generally accompanied by 14 year olds who know, not only how to program in C++, but who are currently on juvenile probation for having hacked their way into the National Security Council computer system.)

You'll probably fall somewhere in the middle. You've bought or somehow gotten access to a computer system. You know just enough to turn it on and watch the system boot up, and maybe even know how to start up a word processing program...but that's about it.

But you want to know more, right?

It's okay at this point even if you don't know a thing about computers because, a little later in the chapter, we'll be walking through the process of booting up your computer and opening the programs step-by-step.

But before we actually start up, let's talk a bit about that round thing included with the book - *The Digital Crystal Ball* CD-ROM.

What is a CD-ROM, Anyway?

By now, you've guessed that the round disk at the back of the book isn't - contrary to what you might have thought - the Grateful Dead's greatest hits, a drink coaster, a pocket mirror, a high-tech frisbee, or some sort of New Age divination device. It's a CD-ROM.

The CD-ROM that's included with this book contains all the programs mentioned in this book - the best metaphysical programs available - and more. The latest information about what is included on the CD-ROM can be found on the CD-ROM itself as a "read me" file, because CD-ROM production and duplication occurs later than the printing of the physical book.

"Read Me" Files

A "read me" file is a term describing a text file often included with software which gives up-to-the-minute info about the software - changes, addenda, extra information, technical details, etc. Look for the file on the CD-ROM.

On the Mac, it will be called "Read Me First!" and you will access it by simply double-clicking on it.

On the IBM side, you will be looking for a file called "DCBINFO.TXT". You can open and read this file by accessing it either through Windows (discussed in the section called "Zap! You're On the Air") or via DOS.

At the DOS-prompt, enter in the following commands -

`C:\> D: TYPE DCBINFO.TXT`

then press the (RETURN) key.

The contents of "DCBINFO.TXT" will then be displayed on your screen. Alternatively, you can print out the file on your printer by entering in the command:

`C:\> D: PRINT DCBINFO.TXT`

Again, if your CD-ROM drive is not labeled "D," see the information box later in this chapter.

Take out the CD-ROM and look at it (see the last part of this chapter for tips on handling, caring for, and storing CD-ROMs). Do you notice a strong resemblance between it and an audio CD? That's because it basically IS the same thing...the same medium, the same manufacturing process, the same kind of packaging. The only difference between the two is that while audio CDs have high quality music on them, CD-ROMs have software on them.

As a matter of fact, most of you will discover that a nice feature of the CD-ROM player included with your computer is that it will also play your audio CDs as well - a good reason to get a couple of external speakers for your system.

The term CD-ROM stands for "Compact Disc - Read Only Memory." ROM memory can generally be thought of as "retrieve only" memory; you can get information from a ROM source, but you cannot record new information onto it.

You'll hear another term - RAM memory - used a lot when talking about computers, as well. RAM stands for "Random Access Memory" and can basically be thought of as a temporary location in your computer where your programs "load" to operate. Another way to think of it is as a virtual "workspace" for your computer, where programs are opened and files are manipulated. Your computer comes equipped with RAM memory (usually measured in megabytes) that can be expanded by the addition of more RAM chips. Generally speaking, the more RAM you have, the easier and faster it is to run programs on your computer - including the programs included with the book.

Remember, you can read information off of the CD-ROM, but you cannot record to it. Because of the way that a lot of software works, you may be required to copy the programs from the CD-ROM to your hard disk in order to run it on your computer, or to run it at optimum speeds. This is especially true of programs that will allow you to save information, such as birth and chart information on ASTRO for Windows.

Save Early, Save Often

A quick, but important, aside here...you'll hear the phrase "save often" repeated by people who work with computers a lot. Meditate on this, Grasshopper, because it is likely to be one of the most important pieces of advice you will ever hear about working on a computer. When you physically "save" a file, you are moving the data you are working on (a letter, spreadsheet, a tarot reading, an astrological chart...whatever) from the temporary RAM area of your computer onto either your hard disk, or a floppy disk's memory, which is (more or less) permanent.

Computers are peculiar beasts with even more peculiar senses of humor...they seem to sense what you are doing. They have the horrible habit of crashing and/or locking up at critical points. That letter to your ex that you've just spent the last three hours poring your heart-felt angst into, the complicated mandala drawing that you've been working on, or a particularly insightful numerological reading can disappear - in the wink of an eye - if your computer decides to lock up on you. And generally, the more important the document, the more likely your computer will play pranks on you. We suspect a "divine comedian" somewhere. So, repeat these words after me, mantra-like, and take them to heart....Save often....Save often.....Save often.......Ohm, er, Aummmmmmmm.

Okay, back to the CD-ROM issue. CD-ROM players started entering the market a few years ago, but with the number of titles available out there already (and increasing phenomenally), it's a medium that will be here for a while. Almost all new Macintosh and IBM-type multimedia computers are now sold with CD-ROM drives as standard equipment.

What You Can Do with Your CD-ROM (If You Don't Have a CD-ROM Drive)

1.) You can hang the CD in your window. When the sunlight strikes it, it is not only beautiful, but it could hypnotize you into believing you can run the programs.

2.) Another suggestion is to find a friend with a CD-ROM player who can copy the files over to floppies for you. It will take quite a few disks, so you may want to pick and choose carefully what you transfer from the CD-ROM to floppies. Some programs, like Virtual Tarot, are, in fact, too large to distribute on floppies.

CD-ROM players come in various configurations depending on your needs. Speed is the most common denominator, and as of the publishing of this book, a "double speed" CD-ROM player appears to be the most common variety available, and the speed to which most CD-ROM publishers are gearing their software towards.

The Virtual Tarot CD-ROM (by Virtual Media Works - see Illustration 2A) is a good example of a multimedia-based, metaphysical software application available on CD-ROM which combines high-quality graphics, sound, music, animation, and compressed video clips. The combination creates a satisfying, multi-sensory "texture" which is quite engaging and contributes considerably to the effectiveness of the "experience" of using the software to perform Tarot readings. The

Illustration 2A. Opening Screen from Virtual Tarot CD-ROM.

Virtual Tarot Demo included on your *Digital Crystal Ball* CD-ROM gives you samples of the animation, audio, and even some video clips.

The CD (Compact Disc) medium is showing up in a lot of applications. Many commercial software packages now include CD-ROMs instead of floppies because of the sheer volume of information CD-ROMs can store. You'll be seeing a lot more CD-ROMs in the future, so pat yourself on the back for having made the oh-so-wise decision to get a CD-ROM player. Think of yourself as a pioneer, without the usual arrows in your back.

The Care and Feeding of CD-ROMs

CD-ROMs are read by laser beams…scary thought, eh?

Don't worry, the lasers in CD-ROM players are generally harmless, so don't be concerned about a stray laser beam escaping the player and slicing you to ribbons or something…it just won't happen. BUT, if for whatever weird reason you happen to find yourself exposed to the business end of the laser reading mechanism, DO NOT look into the beam as it can cause damage to your eyes.

Basically, the information that is on the disk is read by a beam of light reflected off the mirrored surface of the CD-ROM (actually composed of millions of microscopic indentations). The information is then translated into the familiar bits and bytes that computers use to run programs, display graphics, make sounds, show video and animation, etc.

Because of the fragile nature of this "laser-beam-reflects-off-the-microscopic-indentations" transaction, it is best if you handle the disks gently and keep them clean...so, in a nutshell, keep the tofu and bean curd sandwiches in the other room, okay?

In general, to keep your CD-ROMs (and audio CDs for that matter) in tip-top shape, be sure to follow these basic guidelines:

 Handle the disks only by the edges...keep your greasy fingers off of them!

 Don't let them stack up on your desk where they can get scratched or dirty. Put them back in their protective sleeves or jewel cases when they're not being used.

 If they get dusty or dirty, clean them GENTLY with a soft lintless cloth, wiping from the center of the CD-ROM out. Use a little distilled water or similar agent-free cleaner if you absolutely must. Avoid any kind of commercial kitchen cleanser, or anything that might 'melt' or distort the plastic.

There are special commercial cleansing fluids and gadgets available on the market which clean CDs. If it makes you feel better to plop out a few hard-earned dollars to purchase some of this 'paraphernalia' to clean your disks, be my guest. I personally have found that reasonable care and a good clean cloth work just fine.

CD-ROMs, like their counterparts in the music world - the audio CD - are actually pretty tough cookies. But realize that there is a LOT of information stored on them in a very small space. If you've ever attempted to play a damaged audio CD, you know what happens...it skips, or the player simply rejects either the song or the CD altogether.

If handled properly, CD-ROMs, such as the one included with this book, rarely become damaged. But sometimes "stuff happens" and some...or all...of the data on the disk becomes unreadable by the CD-ROM player.

If you have problems with the CD-ROM:

 Try first to clean the disk. Often a gentle cleaning will eliminate the problem.

● Make sure your CD-ROM player is working correctly. Load a known good CD-ROM to make sure the problem is with the disk, and not a player malfunction.

● If you can't get your computer to recognize the CD-ROM at all, it's possible that you are missing a critical piece of software called a "driver" which tells the computer how to operate the CD-ROM player and how to move data from the CD-ROM into your computer. Check your system to make sure a CD-ROM driver has been properly installed.

What's On the Digital Crystal Ball CD-ROM?

IBM

When you load the *Digital Crystal Ball* disc into the CD-ROM player built into your IBM (or compatible) or attached to it as a peripheral, the programs discussed in the book are all located in a directory named DCBALL. Look specifically for file in the directory titled DCBINFO.TXT and view the contents. It will contain information which may have changed regarding files on the CD-ROM since the writing of the book. This might include upgrades, errata, or additional information that is important to the operating of the programs.

Specifically included for the IBM on the *Digital Crystal Ball* CD-ROM are demo and shareware programs for each category of divination mentioned - Astrology, I Ching, Numerology, and Tarot. You'll also find a directory called GOODIES which contains other utilities, programs, etc. that are either supplementary to the key programs included, or that we felt were generally fun and in the spirit of the theme of the book.

On the CD-ROM, inside the directory called DCBALL, you'll find the following offerings for the IBM:

Astrology - *Astro for Windows* is a full-featured astrological program which is shareware by Christopher Noyes. This program allows the user to enter in birth data for individuals, and have the ability to develop - for either on screen viewing or for print - natal charts and in-depth interpretations of a person's profile based on accepted astrological practices, and also to do comparisons between two individuals.

I Ching - *Synchronicity* (demo version) is a product of Synchronicity Software. It allows you to cast the I Ching and create hexagrams and readings that can be read on screen. This demo version has most features of the full version, but does not allow printing or saving.

Numerology - *Personal Numerologist* and *Intimacy* are the two shareware numerology programs by Widening Horizons available for the IBM user. Personal Numerologist allows you to prepare individual deliniations (numerological interpretations) for individuals, and Intimacy allows you to prepare numerologically-based comparison reports for two different people - friends, spouses, and significant others of all flavors and persuasions.

Tarot - *Virtual Tarot* (demo version) is a demo version of the CD-ROM product developed by Virtual Media Works. It allows the viewer to perform a Celtic Cross spread with full audio interpretation. This version lists many of the features of the full commercial product and gives examples of the numerous animations, menus, journal entry screens, and video clips found on the full program.

Macintosh

The CD-ROM included with this book has its own icon which appears on the Finder desktop when you load it into the CD-ROM player built into your Macintosh (or clone), or attached to it as a peripheral. Look for the icon on your desktop (called *Digital Crystal Ball*) and double-click on it to open the CD-ROM and access its contents. Inside you will find folders and files which are the programs mentioned in this book. Look specifically for an icon titled "Read Me First!" and double-click on it. It will contain information which may have changed regarding files on the CD-ROM since the writing of the book. This might include upgrades, errata, or additional information that is important to the operating of the programs.

Specifically included for the Macintosh on the *Digital Crystal Ball* CD-ROM are demo and shareware programs for each category of divination mentioned - Astrology, I Ching, Numerology, and Tarot - as well as a folder called "Goodies" which contains other software that is either supplementary to the key programs included, or are some fun things that we felt you'd like to see and play with.

On the CD-ROM, you find the following offerings for the Mac:

Astrology - *Visions* (demo version) is a full working version of the commercial program by Lifestyle Software Group (all functions work but it does not print or save). Charts can be displayed on screen and both natal and daily horoscopes are available for viewing.

I Ching - *Synchronicity* (demo version) is a product of Synchronicity Software. It allows you to cast the I Ching and create hexagrams and readings that can be seen on screen. This demo version has most features of the full version, but does not allow printing or saving.

Numerology - *Prime* is a numerology shareware program by Harold Feist which is allows for in-depth numerological analysis of a person's name birthdate, address, etc., and will allow you to do numerological comparisons between two individuals. This version of the program will not allow printing reports (but will allow you to save information on individuals), but can be upgraded to the full version which does allow printing and other features, as well.

Tarot - *Virtual Tarot* (demo version) is a demo version of the CD-ROM product developed by Virtual Media Works. It allows the viewer to perform a Celtic Cross spread with full audio interpretation. This version lists many of the features of the full commercial product and gives examples of the numerous animations, menus, journal entry screens, and video clips found on the full program.

Explore...

After you've loaded and accessed the directory or folder level of the CD-ROM, you are essentially ready to explore the various programs and demos available. You cannot damage or erase the files on the CD-ROM, so do not hesitate to poke around and see what's there.

Ladies And Gentlemen...Start Your Engines!

Okay, enough preliminaries! In this section, we'll look at starting up your computers - either the Macintosh, or an IBM PC or clone.

This section will give you a brief (i.e., very short, limited, truncated, necessarily tiny...small) but accurate and sufficient introduction to starting your computers. There are lots of books and tutorials out there to assist those of you new to computers to operate your machines. Very likely, you were provided with detailed introductory manuals when you bought your computer, and most likely you'll find on-line tutorial programs available on your computer to teach you the basics, should you so desire.

So, rather than spend your time going through the minutiae of computer operation, we'll talk just briefly about powering up your computers, and getting you quickly to the level of your computer's "desktop" where you can access the CD-ROM programs. That is what you want to do anyway, isn't it?

A Few Words about Hardware Requirements

In a perfect world, there would be no need for technicians or explanation on how to operate your computer.

Unfortunately though, any technology as complex as computers does require a little explanation, but trust me - we'll try to keep it short here.

There are literally dozens of different IBM clones available, and a few Macintosh clones, too. The directions given in this book address using both 'official' IBMs and Macintoshes, and clones as well.

We're going to have to delve (albeit briefly) into a few details of your computer to make sure that your particular system is up-to-date enough and equipped with the right software and hardware do-dads to properly run the software on the CD-ROM.

In Appendix A, we've listed the system requirements in detail for both Macintosh and IBM/compatibles. Refer to it if you're curious, or if you have a problem. The following is a 'short list' of system requirements which should suffice for 95% of you.

IBM-PCs and Compatibles

- 386 processor or higher (note: some programs will run on a 286 as well)

- DOS and Windows 3.1, or Windows 95

- VGA monitor (256 colors) minimum

- Sound Blaster card or equivalent recommended (for some programs)

- CD-ROM drive

- CD-ROM driver software

Macintosh

(Note: Many of the programs included will run on a simple MacPlus, SE, or SE/30 running system 6.05 or higher, but the following configuration is recommended to view all the programs.)

- Mac LC or higher

- 5 megabytes of application (RAM) memory

System 7.0.1 or above recommended - QuickTime is necessary to play any video segments (version 1.6 or higher)

 CD-ROM drive (single speed supported but double speed is recommended)

 Color capability recommended - 13" monitor capable of displaying 256 colors

 Sound - built in or external speakers

 CD-ROM driver software (if cache capable, it is suggested that approximately 3 Megabytes be allocated for smooth access to the CD-ROM)

System Assumptions - Software Requirements

For the sake of consistency, we make the following assumptions about your computers and the way the software (in particular, the operating systems) is currently configured:

IBM: We assume that your machine is configured with at least Windows 3.1 (which means DOS is also included on your IBM or clone) and that your start-up files are configured to get you either to the Windows desktop (i.e., Program Manager level) or to a DOS "C-prompt" when your computer is turned on and goes through the start-up sequence. This is the traditional way IBMs and their clones come configured from computer stores and resellers, and most likely the way your computer is configured as well. It is assumed that Windows is located in a directory called "WINDOWS" on the "C" drive.

Many users will be upgrading to Windows 95, or will have purchased new machines that come with Windows 95 pre-installed. If you are one of these users, your machine will take you directly to Windows 95 on startup.

Also we assume that the proper software driver (the software that allows the computer and CD-ROM player to 'talk' to each other) is installed for your CD-ROM drive, and that the CD-ROM drive is designated to be drive "D". (See the box later in this chapter if your CD-ROM drive is labeled other than D.)

If you do not see either the DOS prompt (`c:\>`) or the Windows desktop after you turn on your computer and let it completely boot up, then there is likely something wrong with your startup configuration file, or with the hardware of the computer itself. Consult a technician or a knowledgeable 12-year old at that point.

Macintosh: We assume that your System software (we recommend 7.1 or higher) is properly installed and that it boots up to the Finder desktop level, and that the proper software driver for your CD-ROM drive is installed. If your Mac does not boot up properly, it means there may be a problem with your system software installation or a hardware problem - again, consult a technician, or see if the 12-year old mentioned above speaks both IBM and Mac.

Turning the Key on Your "Divination Instruments" - Starting Your Computers

Okay, let's look at turning on your computer. You may not (probably won't as a matter of fact) want to read about starting the "other" platform. Simply skip to the section (IBM or Macintosh) that pertains to you and read it. We'll address the IBM side first - and then the Macintosh.

Zap! Your IBM is on the Air! (Starting the IBM)

Again, working off the assumption that you have Windows 3.1 or Windows 95 installed already, go ahead and start up your computer by turning on the power switch. (It is a good idea to have the CD-ROM loaded in the player at this time, although you can load it later.)

Your computer will then go through a "boot up" process - loading the software into the memory, performing diagnostics on the internal hardware, etc. -

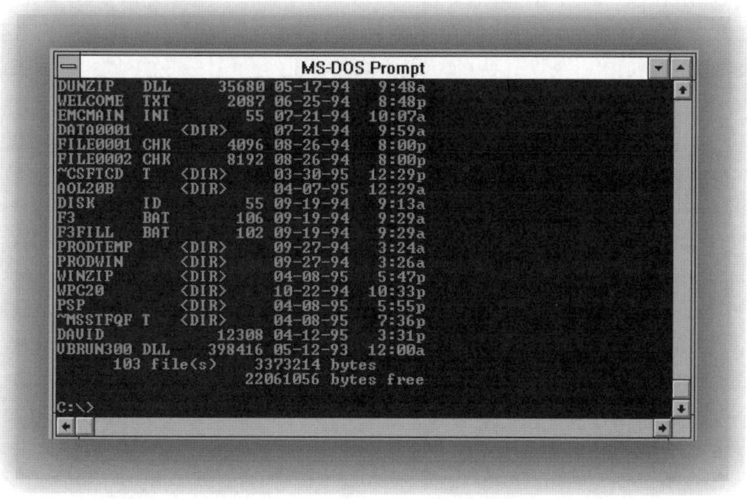

Illustration 2B. The "C-prompt" in the DOS window.

and finally either result in a "C-prompt" or a Windows desktop, as shown in the accompanying illustrations.

MS-DOS Boot up: If you have Windows 95 on your computer, please skip directly to the "Windows 95 Boot Up" section below. But if your computer boots up to the traditional MS-DOS "C-prompt," then the first order of business is to get to the Windows 3.1 "Program Manager" or desktop. This is accomplished by entering in the following command after the "C-prompt":

`C:\> WINDOWS\WIN`

Hit the (RETURN) or (ENTER) key after typing in the command and the Windows desktop will appear in just a few moments. At that point, follow the commands as outlined for the Windows 3.1 boot up below.

Windows 3.1 Boot up: Let's look now at the case where your PC boots up directly to Windows 3.1.

After the opening screen (with the characteristic Windows logo), you will arrive ultimately at the Windows "Program Manager" level as shown in Illustration 2C.

At the Windows "Program Manager" (this 'top' level of the Windows program hierarchy is sometimes referred to as "the desktop") look for the icon called "Main." Click on it to get to the utilities inside; specifically, we're looking for the utility called "File Manager."

File Manager is a very useful utility under Windows. With it, we can look at the content of directories (they're the icons that look like little folders), create or delete directories, create or move files and directories around, and perform other computer housekeeping chores. It is from the File Manager that you can do much of the manipulation of the CD-ROM programs, including copying them to directories on the hard disk. At the bottom of the File Manager window is information which tells you the size of your files, and the disk space on your hard disk.

Clicking on File Manager brings up a graphical representation of your computer's directory and file hierarchy, as well as the structure of directories on external media such as floppies or CD-ROMs. You'll note little icons on the horizontal bar just above the area where you see the folders. These icons (labeled "a", "b", "c", etc.) are your system directories. You will likely see one that looks like it has a CD-ROM being inserted into it - this is your CD-ROM directory.

If the CD-ROM icon is not showing, it means that either you haven't inserted the CD-ROM into the CD-ROM player, or that there may be another problem. If you haven't inserted the CD-ROM yet, do so at this time and let it come up to speed. Select the (F5) function key (do this any time you make a change using File Manager to show the 'new' layout of your directories and files) and you should now see the CD-ROM icon appear.

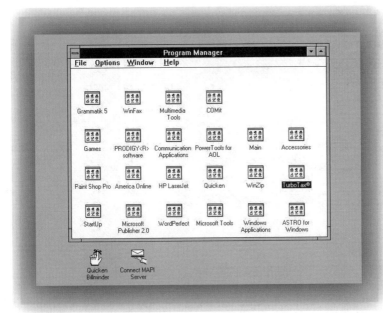

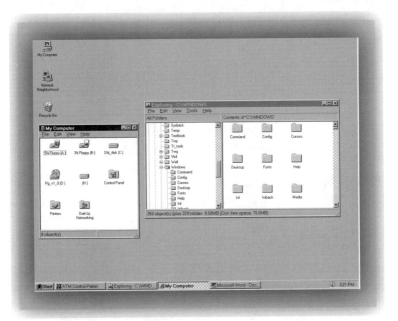

Illustration 2C. The Windows 3.1 Program Manager (top) and the desktop of Windows 95 (bottom), showing My Computer and Explorer.

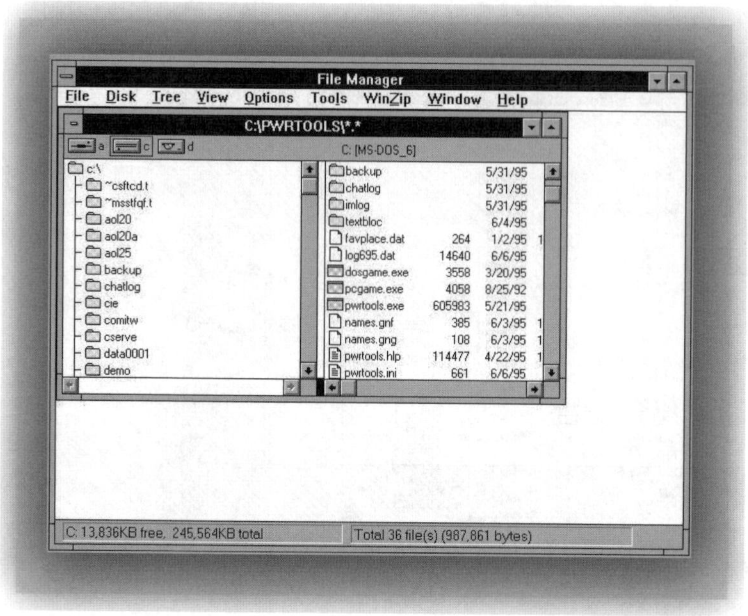

File Manager window showing C:\PWRTOOLS*.* directory listing

Illustration 2D. The File Manager is a useful utility for managing files in Windows. Notice the file and dsk size information at the bottom of the window.

Note to see what letter is directly to the right of the CD-ROM icon. Most likely it is "d" which means your computer is calling the CD-ROM drive "d" (case is unimportant - "d" is the same as "D").

Alright - at this point you are properly booted up, your File Manager is open, and your CD-ROM is loaded and properly identified (as "D" or whatever). You're actually ready to start running a few of the programs.

Windows 95 Boot up: In some ways, using Windows 95 is almost more like using the Macintosh then the previous version of Windows. While you can still use the Windows menu to move and copy files and directories, it's far easier to take advantage of the "drag and drop" features of Windows 95 to move files.

The desktop of Windows 95 includes icons labeled "My Computer" and "Explorer." Like the Windows 3.1 File Manager (see the previous section), they will let you view disks, directories, and files. Make sure the CD-ROM that comes with this book is properly inserted in your PC's CD-ROM drive.

Click to open either My Computer or Explorer. Inside each, you'll see pictorial representations of your hard and floppy disk drives and, hopefully, an icon that shows your CD-ROM drive. (If you do not see the CD-ROM drive, reinsert the CD-ROM and press the (F5) key to refresh the screen. If you still do not see

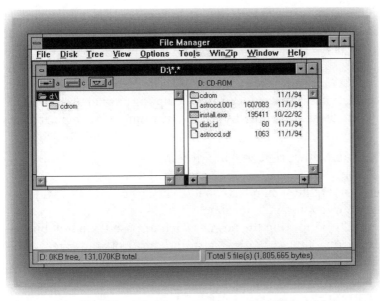

Illustration 2E. The File Manager shows the system drives - note the CD-ROM drive symbol with "d" to the side.

the CD-ROM, see the portions of this chapter that discuss the CD-ROM drive.) A letter next to the CD-ROM icon will tell you how that drive is labeled (for instance, D).

CD-ROM Drives on the IBM....

One piece of information that is important for you to know is how your IBM or compatible addresses the CD-ROM drive. In the IBM world, all disk drives (hard drives, floppies, and CD-ROMs) are addressed with an alphabetical reference (in either upper or lowercase, case is not an important issue). The main system drive (the one with the DOS and Windows directories on it) is generally referenced as the "C" drive, the first floppy drive is designated as the "A" drive, and other drives are designated as "B," "D," "E," "F," and so on. The CD-ROM drive is usually labeled as drive "D," and that is what we will assume in this book (again, either "d" or "D" is acceptable).

If you find that your CD-ROM is named something different than "d" (for instance "e" or "f" or "g"), please make note of that difference and substitute the letter designating your CD-ROM in the following install directions and also any time you see "d" (or "D") designated in a command that you are directed to enter.

If you feel you need more assistance or wish to learn more about how to use the keyboard, mouse, or other aspects of interfacing with your PC, consider going through one of the online tutorials that likely came with your computer.

Read the previous section in the book called "What's On the Digital Crystal Ball CD-ROM?" to look at the contents of the CD-ROM itself. Skip over the next section (which addresses Macintosh startup) to learn about copying programs from the CD-ROM in order to run them on your individual IBM or compatible computer.

Boot 'em up, Mac...Starting the Macintosh

For those of you with Macintosh computers, the world is a pretty simple place. Although it isn't quite as simple as double-clicking on an icon and you're on line divining your fool head off, it's almost that easy.

When you first "boot up" (flip the power switch or push the on-off button) you'll see the small "happy face" Mac icon in the center of your screen. This means the Macintosh is ready to load the operating system (the computer code

Illustration 2F. Typical Mac icons representing hard drives, files, programs, "trash," etc.

or set of commands that make the Macintosh operate) from either a floppy disk or - more likely - your hard disk.

Once the machine finds the operating system, the happy face is replaced by a box which says "Welcome to Macintosh." (This has changed in System 7.5 and beyond. The new "MacOS" logo is displayed following the "Welcome to Macintosh" box that has been around for more than a decade).

The Mac is automatically doing several things at this point, including loading the System software (including fonts, assorted "utilities", etc.), checking the computer's integrity (e.g., the memory, video, etc.), and opening the next screen called the "Finder."

The Finder is the top level of the Mac and can be thought of as a 'desktop' where you do your work with the Mac - running programs, creating and saving files, putting things in folders, doing your online divination, etc.

On the desktop you'll see several little pictures called "Icons." One represents your hard disk, another represents the "trash", and there may be others as well. If you placed the *Digital Crystal Ball* CD-ROM in your CD-ROM drive, it is likely that you'll see its icon on your desktop as well.

The mouse-controlled movable arrow on the screen - combined with the keyboard - represents your interface to the Mac and the programs on both the CD-ROM as well as the other programs on your hard disk. By moving the mouse around and clicking the icons, you'll have access to the programs and files, and also have the ability to make selections, move files and folders around, etc.

If you are not comfortable using the mouse, or feel that you need more orientation to the operation of the Mac way of navigating around a computer, you may want to go through some of the tutorials which were included with your computer and were likely loaded with your Mac operating system.

Apple has created some marvelous training tools to orient owners and Mac "neophytes." Check inside your hard disk to see if a tutorial folder is present. Simply drag the arrow over the icon representing the hard disk and do a quick "double-click" with the mouse button. The hard disk icon will open up another window on your Finder's desktop which shows you its contents. Look for a folder called "Macintosh Tutorial" or a similar name. See how it works? You've just completed lesson number one!

Copying Programs from the CD-ROM to your Hard Disk

Some of the applications on the CD-ROM will need to be copied to your hard disk to operate properly, or you may simply wish to put them there for easy access or performance improvement (i.e., they'll run more quickly).

Copying CD-ROM files using the IBM

Copying programs and directories from the CD-ROM to your IBM's hard disk is a pretty straightforward process. As you progress through the book, you'll find directions which tell how to copy programs using DOS, but for now, we'll focus on copying programs and directories using the File Manager of Windows 3.1, or the Explorer or My Computer icons of Windows 95.

If you're using Windows 3.1, open the "Main" program group on your Program Manager and double-click on the File Manager icon. This will bring up the characteristic split-screen display (directories on left, files on right) of the File Manager.

The top horizontal bar (sometimes referred to as the "drive bar") of the File Manager displays icons which represent the drives available to you; look for and select the icon that looks like a drive with a small CD-ROM inserted into it. This is the icon which will give you access to the directory of the *Digital Crystal Ball* CD-ROM (most likely labeled as drive D). Click on it with your mouse to make it the "active" directory (a small box will appear around the icon). Select (F5) from the 'function keys' at the top of your keyboard to 'refresh' the File Manager (do this any time you select a drive or directory to display the 'new' contents on the File Manager display).

On the left hand side of the File Manager screen, you will then see little 'folders' which represent the directories of the CD-ROM. To see the directory contents, click on one of the folders (ASTROLGY, NUMRLOGY, ICHING, or TAROT) and you will see additional small folders appear underneath these main folders/directories. For instance, if you select NUMRLOGY, you will find the folders PERSONAL and INTIMACY appear, which are the sub-directories holding the files for Personal Numerologist and Intimacy respectively.

Select the folder representing the directory you wish to copy with your mouse; then go to the File menu, select it with your mouse and look for and select "Copy..."

A dialog box comes up on your screen as shown below (Illustration 2G), into which you will be entering the destination that you wish the directory to be copied to (typically, this is drive C, so enter in the letter "C" if you wish to copy to your "C" drive).

Then select the "OK" button with your mouse or simply hit the (ENTER) or (RETURN) button on your keyboard. This tells your computer to go to the CD-ROM (called "D" in this case) and to hunt for and select the directory you wish to copy, and to copy it to your "C" drive (your 'main' hard drive). See Illustration 2G for an example of the copy command as entered in the File Manager.

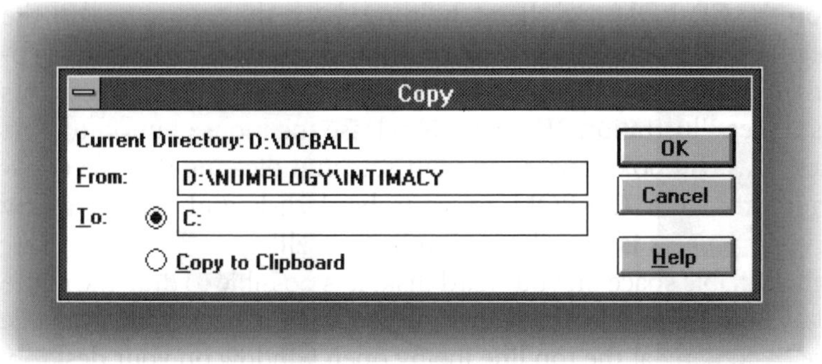

Illustration 2G. From the "Copy..." selection under the File menu in the File Manager of Windows 3.1, you can direct your computer to copy a directory from your CD-ROM onto your hard disk. The example shown is for copying the INTIMACY directory from drive D to drive C.

If you're using Windows 95, you can copy files in a similar way to Windows 3.1. In 95's My Computer or Windows Explorer, click on the CD-ROM drive to access the *Digital Crystal Ball* CD-ROM. Click to open the CD and view its directory and files. Click on the file or folder you want to copy. Select "Copy" from the Edit menu. Open the folder or disk where you want to put the copy. On the Edit menu, click "Paste." If you'd like to select more than one file or folder to copy, hold down the (CTRL) key, and then click the items you want.

So, for instance, if you want to copy the Numerology programs to your hard disk, click the NUMRLOGY folder on your CD-ROM. Select "Copy" from the Edit menu and then click on your hard disk. Then select "Paste." The Numerology folder and all files and folders within it will be copied to your C: drive.

But there is an easier way to copy files using Windows 95:

In My Computer or Windows Explorer, find the file or folder on the CD-ROM you want to copy. Make sure the place you want to drag the file or folder to (most likely your hard disk) is visible. Drag the file or folder to the destination disk. If you are dragging a directory, all files and subdirectories within it will be copied. Easy, eh?

Note that if you use your right mouse button to drag, a menu will appear with the available options.

Copying CD-ROM files using the Macintosh

To copy a folder from the CD-ROM to your hard disk, you simply click on the icon of the folder containing the program application (or applications) you

etc.), or through other means, such as the CD-ROM included with this book. They do this in the hope that you will like their programs enough to pay for them.

Shareware developers are generally entrepreneurial-types who simply don't have the resources to go through the traditional (and expensive) production and distribution channels to sell their software. Often they develop products which are highly specialized, appealing to a more limited market - such as some of the divination tools included on your CD-ROM.

The idea behind Shareware is that, once you try a shareware program and you find it useful to you, then you'll be honest and pay the programmer who did the work a little something for his effort - so that he can afford to do it again. The shareware authors do not make any money directly from this book. They have graciously allowed us to distribute their programs - so please, we encourage you to register your shareware.

Don't get the idea that shareware is schlockware; the quality of many shareware programs meets or exceeds that of commercial programs. In fact, many commercial programs on the shelves today started out originally being distributed as shareware. The shareware programs we've chosen for this book are as good as any commercial programs available.

The big question of course is - why bother to support shareware?

Lots of practical reasons, actually...

Many shareware programs are distributed like commercial demos - only partially functional; registering your shareware program gives you a fully functional program, and often gets you the latest version of the program as well (often old versions of shareware programs float around the computer community for years). Also, registration of shareware will often get you documentation, on-line support by the developer, notices of new releases, etc.

A couple of more indirect, but important things to consider regarding shareware...

By paying shareware fees, you are supporting a budding software community. You don't need a calculator to realize that the price being asked by shareware developers for their products is often hundreds of dollars less than commercial programs - with comparable and often better quality. By selling directly to you, the shareware developers eliminate all the middle men, and give to you what you want - a program - not a bunch of expensive four-color cardboard packaging and shrinkwrap plastic that is summarily tossed in the trash.

Microsoft doesn't sell astrology or I Ching programs for a reason - the market is too small. Supporting shareware developers makes it possible to bring specialized programs (such as divination programs) to the market. Face it - you don't just wake up one morning and say, "I think today I'll just whip out a fully-functional Astrology program with full ephemeris calculation features, color charting capability and complete interpretation ability *and* on-line help." It takes a special kind of commitment to produce a program like that. Software isn't free - anymore than music is free, artwork is free, books are free, or food is free.

Commercial Demos

In an effort to entice you to buy their products, commercial software developers often release demo versions of their products which are, in some manner, "less" than the real thing - not all the features work or are fully operable. They don't save, they don't print, they only operate for thirty days, or some other "crippling" scheme is programmed into them.

The idea of a "demo" is not unlike a first date - hopefully you'll like them enough that you'll want to make a "commitment." In essence, you have the opportunity to "test drive" the software - to see if it's for you. This is a great concept for getting a "feel" for a program and its inherent usefulness (or lack of same) to you. There are several excellent commercial demos on the CD-ROM included with this book. Hopefully after trying them, you'll find them useful to you, and you'll consider the benefits of buying the full-blown programs.

No Free Lunches

A last thought on shareware and really, software in general - software is intellectual property and shares many of the same inherent traits as music, artwork, and books - one being that it's easily reproducible. Generally speaking, any 11-year old of average intelligence can defeat your basic software copy protection scheme with a utility and a few keystrokes.

A software program is not simply a product, but also a symbol representing hundreds of hours of somebody's programming and development efforts (or in the case of more complex packages - several "somebodies"). And behind that effort is a lot of expertise - education, experience and ideas - which, in the cosmic scheme of things, is worth quite a lot of energy.

Remember that it's a zero-sum universe out there. There are no free lunches - you *will* reap what you sow.

So, the next time you have a flat at 3 A.M. on a deserted road in the rain, and you go back to the trunk only to discover that the spare is down and you left the jack back in the garage as well, maybe you'll stop and ponder whether or not you're possibly overdrawn at the Karmic Savings and Loan.

Pay your shareware fees. Trust me - you'll sleep better for it.

Seeking Additional Support

In this book, we've tried to strike a compromise - enough detail to get you up and running, but not enough "computerese" to bog you down and steer you away from the real reason you bought the book anyway - to delve into online divination.

Our hope is that you'll have no problems at all, but we're not naive enough to believe you won't hit a snag - sooner or later.

Our suggestion is that, should you run into a problem - either with the software (on either the CD-ROM or in your computer) or your hardware - the first order of business is to breathe deeply, walk away from the computer, go outside and pull a few weeds, fix yourself a nice cup of tea, read a poem from "Leaves of Grass" - you get the idea. The main thing is - do not freak out.

If you're having problems with the software, re-read (or simply *read*) the section in the book covering it; perhaps you've missed a critical detail. Or, perhaps the detail was overlooked (we're good, but not infallible). Included with most of the programs is either a manual (which you may be able to print out) or there is on-line help available in the program itself. Check the menus for help and look in directories and folders of the CD-ROM for possible manuals or other information found on "read me" files there.

Other ideas? If your computer is under warranty, you likely have phone support available to you. The manuals that came with your computers offer lots of trouble-shooting information, and there are a plethora of good books available at your library or local bookstores to help you deal with common computer problems.

A computer savvy friend might be helpful. Offer to cast his (or her) natal chart, or allow them to sit down and consult the I Ching.

And then there's the local 15-year-old whizkid (yours perhaps?) who understands computers inside and out...a little bartering may be in order. Find out who she or he has a crush on and offer to "check out their compatibility" (for a modest outlay of assistance on their part, of course).

Neither LightSpeed Publishing nor the author can provide phone support. Those with internet access can send email to the publishers at help@LSP.com and they will do their best to help you. There may even be software updates (or additional offerings) and/or some answers available to commonly asked questions.

If you suspect that the problem is hardware related, consult a certified technician or repair facility to check out the situation.

Common Problems and Solutions

The following is a short list of common problems encountered by computer users of all types. It's not intended to be complete, but covers some typical problems you might encounter with possible solutions.

⚫ **Nothing's happening**

Make sure the power cord is plugged into the wall; you have no idea how often it happens that the computer is simply not plugged in. Check out all cables, power and otherwise, for proper connection, and to make sure the cables themselves are good. Repair or replace bad cables. Are you sure the outlet you've plugged into works? And the wall switch is on?

⚫ **There's no sound**

Check to make sure the volume is up on your speaker(s); this might be either controlled manually by a volume control on the speaker itself, or via a software control.

Sound capability is built into the Macintosh, but sound playback capability generally requires a separate sound board on IBMs and compatibles.

⚫ **No picture on the monitor or monitor problems in general**

Monitors generally have a *separate* power cord from the CPU; check to assure that it is plugged in and turned on. Also make sure that the cable from the monitor to the CPU is present and properly connected. Check the brightness and contrast knobs on your monitor, too.

⚫ **The CD-ROM isn't working...**

Several possibilities here - the hardware might not be working properly (if it is an external drive, check that it is properly powered and that it is properly cabled to the CPU); the software driver might not be properly installed (if at all), or might simply be corrupted; or the drive itself may be in need of alignment. Consult the manuals that came with your CD-ROM player for details.

Additionally, review the information presented earlier in this book concerning handling and care of your CD-ROMs. Maybe the CD-ROM needs a little cleaning to work properly.

PART TWO

Online Insights - The Programs

I n this section of *The Digital Crystal Ball,* we'll look at operating the divination programs included with this book. ❷ The Part is divided into four chapters, one for each of the divination methods - Astrology, Tarot, I Ching, and Numerology. ❷ You can choose the one which appeals to you most and immediately go to it at anytime...so take a reading of your psyche and see which way it's gravitating.

Each chapter provides an introduction to a type of divination and has complete operating instructions for the major programs included on the CD-ROM. We'll first discuss how the IBM program operates, and then we'll check out the Macintosh program - and you'll see that this convention is followed throughout the four chapters.

Take your time, read carefully through the pages and be sure to look for additional help provided by the developers of the programs in either on-line help files, "read me" files, or even sometimes in manuals for the programs that you can print out.

So dim the lights and light the incense. Tie a gypsy scarf around your neck, loosen up those fingertips and explore, experiment, and generally indulge yourself...you might discover there's a cosmic e-mail message out there with your name on it, just waiting for you!

Just don't make a nuisance of yourself bugging your friends for their birthdates...okay?

IMPORTANT PC NOTICE

We strongly recommend that you install and run the DOS programs (Synchronicity, Personal Numerologist, and Intimacy) under DOS instead of through Windows.

If these programs do not run and give you an error message saying the files are locked, go into the directory you created for each DOS program and type:

```
attrib-r *.*
```

Then start the program again.

3

The Online Astrologer

"Astrology is a science in itself and contains an illuminating body of knowledge. It taught me many things, and I am greatly indebted to it. Geophysical evidence reveals the power of the stars and the planets in relation to the terrestrial. In turn, astrology reinforces this power to some extent. This is why astrology is like a life-giving elixir for mankind."

-Albert Einstein

What Is Astrology? The Call of the Night Sky...

I decided to make the drive at night - the occasional bad AM radio station and the lights from my dashboard were my only companions as I drove the 500 desolate miles of West Texas desert that stretches between Carlsbad, NM and San Antonio.

It was late August - the night air of a particularly hot Texas summer passed through the open car window and combined with the hypnotically repetitious pattern of white dashes on the highway, putting me into a kind of trance - a heightened sense of awareness of myself and of my surroundings. At about 2:30 in the morning, I pulled the car over to the edge of the road and got out to stretch my cramped legs. I was completely alone, the last car had past me several miles before, and the lights of the last farmhouse left far in the distance over the last set of hills.

As my eyes slowly adjusted to the all-encompassing darkness, what met me was an awe-inspiring sight...something that, as your basic urban dweller, I'd never before seen with such clarity. Emblazoned across the sky were the jewels of the Zodiac - constellations, and literally millions of stars - stretching from horizon to horizon with the Milky Way holding them in place like a banner against the blue-blackness of the wide Texas sky.

As countless millions of others had done before me - over tens of thousands of years - I stood there and silently contemplated my place in the universe, and considered the influence of the heavens on my rather insignificant form - standing alone in the desert - on a tiny outpost planet at the edge of the galaxy that I considered my home. At a subconscious level, I was sharing an experience that I knew was as old as mankind - and as equally profound.

From the beginning of history, humans have had a fascination with the heavens, its visible satellites, and their influence upon them.

Artifacts from the Old Stone Age give evidence that prehistoric man very likely practiced a primitive form of Astrology. The first serious Astrological studies appear to have been done by the Sumerians - the world's oldest recognized civilization. The Sumerians studied and practiced Astrology around 4300 BC, exclusively to predict and interpret the events in the lives of royalty. As time went on, the practice and study of Astrology grew, with evidence of its study found in elaborate observatories and monuments in the diverse cultures of Meso-America, India, Persia, Africa, and Western Europe, just to mention a few. The first evidence of its use by the general populace occurred in Greece sometime around the second century BC.

In reality, much of what gets passed off today as Astrology is a watered-down and trivialized fortune-telling activity, for the most part dismissed or ignored by "serious" Astrology students.

These popular 'astrological forecasts' found in virtually every daily newspaper (and increasingly in every genre of magazine) are very general, broad strokes of the astrological pen, focusing only on a small portion of the Astrological cosmos - the twelve "Sun signs" (Gemini, Libra, Aquarius, Scorpio, and so forth).

"Sun Sign Astrology" - as it is commonly called - places everyone into one of only 12 different personality categories, depending upon which part of the zodiac the sun was passing through when you were born. Because it has only 12 different categories for the entire population of the world to fit within, the predictions of Sun Sign Astrology are pretty general and easy to statistically disprove (i.e., One-twelfth of the planet born under the sun sign of Libra won't be getting a raise or meeting their future beloved on Thursday - regardless of what *The Times* says).

Let's Get Sirius, Shall We?

Serious devotees of Astrology are much more methodical and analytical - their interpretation of an individual's destiny starts by consulting the complex inter-relationships of the heavenly bodies via a reference tool called an **ephemeris.**

At the moment of your birth, all the astrologically significant celestial bodies (the planets, the sun, and the moon) were in precise, mathematically calculable positions.

By knowing the exact location of your birth (usually expressed in longitude and latitude), the exact time of your birth, and your birth date, an astrologer (referring to an ephemeris database) can reconstruct an exact model of the heavens that appeared overhead when you were born.

After the chart information is plotted, a skilled astrologer, using a combination of time-honored interpretations (and a touch of intuitive insight), can provide an individual with a view of his life based upon the influence of the planets, the stars, the moon, and the sun.

As you might imagine, this plotting process - calculating the location of each of the eight planets, the Moon and Sun, and relating it all to an exact location on the globe - is your basic proverbial "rocket science" kind of problem; lots and lots of number crunching is involved. And like most "rocket science" problems today, what better way to solve the problem than with a computer?

Included on your CD-ROM are software tools which the early astrologers would have paid dearly for - powerful and complete computerized chart and ephemeris generators that will give you - in a matter of seconds - what would have taken the astrologers of yore days or weeks to calculate using traditional methodologies, and would have filled volumes of books.

These programs (Visions for the Macintosh, and ASTRO for Windows) will allow you to enter personal information into easy-to-fill-out forms and produce for yourself, your family, and friends (on your own computer) the complex astrological charts that many professional astrologers (or clever entrepreneurs) advertise and sell today for $20 to $100 or more.

"Twinkle, Twinkle Little Star" - An Overview of Astrology

Probably more has been written about Astrology than all the other divination tools included in this book and CD-ROM combined. This book doesn't intend to be a definitive astrological guide; there are plenty of excellent texts available at your local bookstore or library which cover the literally hundreds of details about astrology. I've included several excellent references in the appendix and there is more information included in the Help and information areas of the individual programs (be sure to check out the online help files!). But we do provide you with enough information to chart your horoscopes - just enough to make you dangerous (and whet your appetite)!

In many ways - Astrology can be thought of as the 'oldest' and most culturally pervasive divinatory science, with evidence of its study virtually a cliché in the history of almost every culture.

Astrology and Numerology are the two divinatory methodologies included in this book which are generally thought of as "scientific" - i.e., skilled astrologers in two different areas of the world should be able to reproduce similar charts for a given individual, given the same birth information (date and time of birth, and longitude and latitude of the birth location).

The methodologies used by astrologers vary slightly depending on the astrologer and his or her particular opinions, but generally fall into just a few standard approaches, which we'll discuss in a moment.

Is It the Age of Aquarius?

"When the moon is in the seventh house, and Jupiter aligns with Mars, then peace will guide the planets - and love will steer the stars"

- Hair, 1967

If 1967 was the "dawning" of the Age of Aquarius, then I suppose that as we rapidly approach the end of the century, we're at the "second cup of coffee" stage of the era...or maybe not.

What exactly the phrase "Age of Aquarius" means is of some controversy among astrologers. There is agreement that the period that we are moving out of (The Age of Pisces) began about the time of the birth of Christ , but exactly when the Age of Pisces ends - and the Age of Aquarius begins is unclear. Some astrologers say the Age of Aquarius started in 1904, others that we will not officially enter the Age until after the beginning of the next millennium - still others say that it doesn't begin until as late as the twenty-fourth century.

Technically speaking, an astrological "age" is a period of about 2100 years, corresponding (listen carefully) to the length of time that the Sun rises with a particular zodiac constellation on the vernal (or springtime) equinox. In other words, for the last 2000 years (give or take), the sun has risen on the eastern horizon on the first day of Spring along with the constellation Pisces. But - as the gears of the galaxy crank inevitably along - we're slowly creeping into a situation where Pisces is being replaced by Aquarius as the rising sign. Understandably, where the constellation Pisces (and its influence) leaves off and Aquarius begins in the cosmological scheme of things is a trifle vague, even for astrologers - hence the controversy. So...keep those fringed vests and peace signs available in your closet until further notice.

What Can an Astrological Reading Tell Me?

There are similarities between the information that an Astrological reading gives you and other divination methodologies. Information about your relationships, your personality (and its quirks), your career, finances, spirituality, etc., are available to you through interpretation of the charts that are produced by a comprehensive astrology program - such as the ones included on the *Digital Crystal Ball* CD-ROM.

A major difference between astrological readings and other types of divination is that, inherent in the "design" of astrology is the recognition of the changing scope of your life through time, due to the changes in the influences of the cosmos. As such, astrology can be used to predict periods of stress, give specific information about current events in your life (or future or past events), and foretell possible moments of triumph - or possible defeat. Once you've put a chart together, it can be consulted over and over to give you new information about the influence of the stars and planets over your life.

An Astrological Primer

It would be virtually impossible, in just a few pages, for any book to do justice to the myriad processes and approaches used by astrologers (and astrology programs) to devise charts and interpretations for individuals. But let's look at the major types of astrological documents that are produced, in particular those calculated by Visions and ASTRO for Windows.

The primary document which is used by astrologers as a basis for individual interpretation is the **natal chart** or birth chart. This chart is what is normally thought of when an astrologer (or astrology program) "casts a horoscope."

The completed natal chart is essentially a map of the heavens at the moment of birth, interpreted from a precise birth location. It is a unique document, describing - in graphical shorthand - how the Zodiac, the planets, the moon, and the sun were related to each other at the moment of an individual's birth. (It is significant to note that - contrary to popular belief - most astrology techniques do NOT involve the influence of individual stars, per se. It is the planets and their positions that are of chief concern when interpreting celestial influences.)

At the center of the natal chart is the Earth - makes sense doesn't it, considering that's where you were born (most of you, anyway)? Around the Earth are the twelve divisions called "**Houses**" (more on Houses below), arranged equally at 30-degree intervals.

On the IBM version of the program, the signs of the Zodiac are seen on the edge of both the chart on the monitor, as well as the printed chart. The Mac

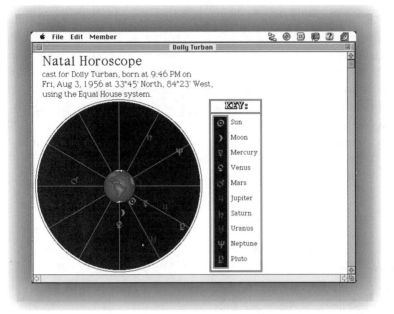

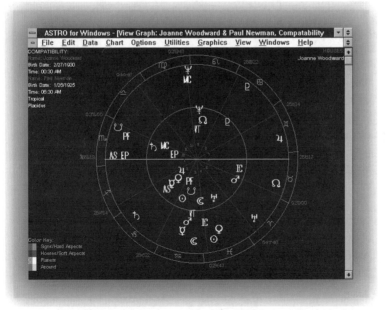

Illustration 3A. Natal charts as displayed onscreen for both the ASTRO for Windows and Visions programs.

program - Visions - produces a highly simplified natal chart with the planets identified in the House locations by their traditional iconographic "glyphs," with all significant relational data listed textually.

Two of the more significant signs on a complete natal chart are the **Ascendant** sign and the **Midheaven** sign. The Ascendant sign is the zodiac sign rising in the East at the time of birth and the Midheaven is the sign directly overhead. Each has significant influences on the personality of the individual.

On the chart, the East horizon is always on the left-hand side and the West horizon is always on the right (just the reverse of maps because we are looking at an "inverted bowl" of the heavens). This places the Ascendant sign at the far left and the Midheaven sign at the top of the chart.

The twelve divisions of the chart, as already mentioned, are commonly referred to as "Houses," with the Ascendant then located at the "cusp" of House 1, and the Midheaven located at the "cusp" of House 10 - a cusp is simply the starting point of a House division. (See Illustration 3B.)

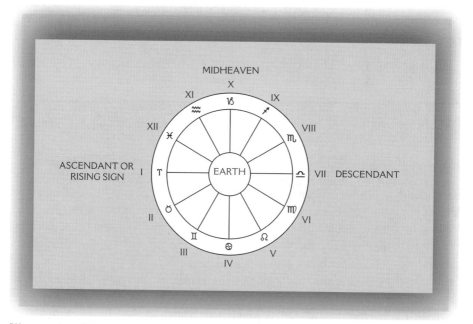

Illustration 3B. Simplified natal chart showing 12 zodiac/house divisions, Ascendant, Midheaven and the Earth.

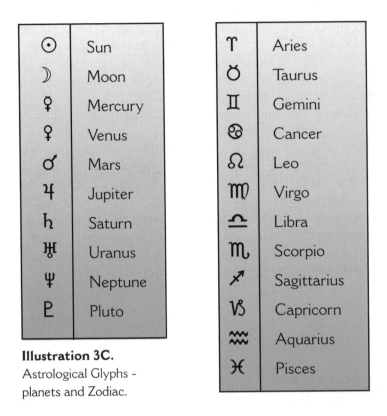

☉	Sun	♈	Aries
☽	Moon	♉	Taurus
☿	Mercury	♊	Gemini
♀	Venus	♋	Cancer
♂	Mars	♌	Leo
♃	Jupiter	♍	Virgo
♄	Saturn	♎	Libra
♅	Uranus	♏	Scorpio
♆	Neptune	♐	Sagittarius
♇	Pluto	♑	Capricorn
		♒	Aquarius
		♓	Pisces

Illustration 3C.
Astrological Glyphs –
planets and Zodiac.

The proper method for determining where the cusps actually begin is a question of some controversy among astrologers. The predominant systems - Placidus (the most common), and Koch - are available on both astrology software programs on the CD-ROM, and charts can be calculated using either system.

The Houses are numbered 1 through 12 counterclockwise (starting at the Ascendant) and can be thought of as a distinct astrological category, relating to an area of life significance, i.e., personality, possessions, education, aspirations, etc.

At this point, you have the basic components of a blank natal chart; it is the task of the astrologer (or the astrology program) to "fill-in" the significant data depending on your birthdate and birth location.

Similar to the Houses, each planet (in astrology, the sun and moon are thought of as planets) has characteristic influences, as well (i.e., Venus is associated with harmony and unity, Mars with initiative, energy, Uranus with change, the Moon with instinct, responsiveness, etc. - see Illustration 3E).

House	Characteristic
1	Personality, Health, Physical Appearance
2	Possessions and attitude towards same
3	Family, School, Mind, Transportation
4	Beginning and end of life, Home, Parents
5	Creativity, Children, Love Affairs, Pets
6	Work, Subordinates, Service
7	Close Relationships, Marriage Partners
8	Money (especially inheritance), Crime
9	Morality, Conscience, Mental Exploration
10	Aspirations, Public Life, Professions
11	Personal Pleasures, Friends, Memberships
12	Limitations, The Unconscious

Illustration 3D. Astrological Houses and simplified listing of their significant issues.

The information for drawing (or "casting") the natal chart is actually determined by referring to very complex set of data called an ephemeris. An ephemeris is a database which gives precise information about the location of planets, zodiac constellations, the moon and sun at a specific time and specific geographical location. Ephemerides (plural for ephemeris) also provide Sidereal time calculations or "Star Time" (not to be confused with "Stardates" a la Star Trek).

The formulae used to calculate the ephemeris databases are *very* complex, involving spherical trigonometry and precise knowledge of the elliptical paths of the celestial bodies. Because of this, you should breathe a sigh of relief that the computer programs on the CD-ROM calculate - within a few seconds - all of this for you.

☉	Sun	Power, Purpose, Vitality
☽	Moon	Responsiveness, Instinct
☿	Mercury	Communications, Mentality
♀	Venus	Harmony and Unity
♂	Mars	Energy, Initiative
♃	Jupiter	Expansiveness, Enthusiasm
♄	Saturn	Limits, Sensitivity
♅	Uranus	Sudden Change, Independence
♆	Neptune	Vagueness, Uncertainty
♇	Pluto	Elimination, Fresh Start

Illustration 3E. Planets and their characteristics.

The aim of the horoscope charting process ultimately then is to get:

- The precise location of all the planets (including the moon and sun)

- Into the zodiac signs at the time of birth (for the individual whose horoscope is being cast)

- And into the right Houses

all taking into consideration the exact location of birth as well. Whew! Aren't you glad the computer does this all for you?

The position of the planets, the signs of the Zodiac and the Houses comprise three of the four main elements of a Horoscope casting.

The fourth element - the **Aspects** - describe the angular and positional relationships between the planets as seen from the Earth. When two planets (including the moon and the sun) are roughly in the same part of the sky on a chart, those planets are said to be in "conjunction" with each other, with their influence and forces merging together. Planets separated by 90-degrees are considered to be "square" and frustrate the influences of each other. Planets 120-

degrees apart, or "trine," work together smoothly, and planets opposite each other (180-degrees) are expressed through contrast.

Once we've placed the planets on the natal chart and calculated the aspects, we're 90% there. We then can use all the information we've gathered to make commentaries about the various aspects of a person's personality, character, and life. This is done by looking at the location of the planets in the zodiac and the Houses, and the associated "aspects" of the planets.

Each planet (in its sign and house) is in a particular aspect relationship to each of the other planets (in their respective signs and houses). These relationships are the foundations of the commentaries astrologers make about an individual's psychological makeup, and other issues of his or her life.

This interpretation process normally involves referencing commentary (usually from texts written by knowledgeable astrologers) about the multitudinous combinations of planets, signs, houses, and aspects. From this "cookbook" approach, an astrologer can develop complex profiles for individuals and note trends when the same interpretations are found in multiple locations within an individual's chart.

The Programs

You'll find IBM-PC and Macintosh programs on the included CD. We'll first describe how to create a detailed Astrology reading using the IBM program so Macintosh users may want to skip ahead to the Mac section.

ASTRO for Windows

ASTRO for Windows is the *Digital Crystal Ball's* offering for the IBM in the category of Astrology. A Windows program, ASTRO is an excellent full-featured horoscope charting and interpretation program developed and distributed by Christopher Noyes, suitable for use by the newcomer to astrology, and the seasoned professional astrologer, as well.

The shareware version included on the CD-ROM is referred to as the "Lite" version, but believe me - it's no lightweight when it comes to features. In fact, there's so many features, I can only cover a few of the more prominent ones in this chapter. Chris is giving you 30 days to look over the program and determine if the quality and features suit your needs. Then, you should think about doing the right thing - registering and paying your shareware fee.

ASTRO for Windows Information

The copy of ASTRO for Windows included with this book is shareware, and as such, readers are asked to use it on a trial basis. If you enjoy the program, its author, Christopher Noyes, requests that you become a registered user. Christopher J. Noyes Software may be reached on CompuServe, America Online, or by fax, phone, or mail. See the program's Registration Form for details.

With ASTRO, you'll be able to quickly produce birth (natal) charts and view them in color on your monitor, as well as print them out. In conjunction with graphical chart development, interpretative textual reports are also produced, giving insightful commentary on an individual's personalities and the influence of planetary aspects. You can even (through the "compatibility" feature) plot two individuals' charts together to look at their compatibility from the astrological point of view.

You can upgrade ASTRO through a sort of "roll your own" process which allows you to add on features as you need them (and as you become more astrologically astute). You only pay for the ones you need or want. Contact Christopher Noyes for details. Information about registration and details on the Deluxe and Professional versions of ASTRO (and the 33,000-city location database) are available on the text files; click on the icons labeled "Versions File," "Registration Form," and "README File" after you have installed the program on your hard disk to get information on registering and upgrades.

Installing ASTRO for Windows

Because you'll want to save information about individuals (birthdates, birth times, and birth locations) that you create horoscope charts for, it's required that you install the ASTRO for Windows program onto your hard disk. This will also create a Program Group for your Windows desktop that will make starting up ASTRO simply a matter of clicking an "ASTRO for Windows" icon. Installing ASTRO for Windows requires approximately 2 megabytes of hard disk space.

To install ASTRO with Windows 3.1, first go to the Windows Program Manager level and select the left-most pulldown menu labeled "**File**." Under File, look for and select "Run..." and enter in the following command exactly as shown into the "Command Line" box. (As mentioned elsewhere in the book,

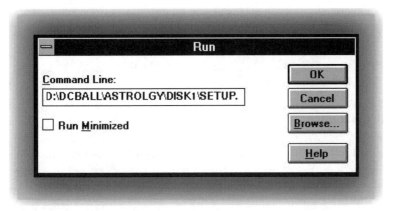

Illustration 3F. Enter the install command for ASTRO into the "Run" command line; the entry will "wrap " as you enter the command.

we assume that your CD-ROM drive is designated as drive "D". If it is different [e.g., "E" or "F"] substitute that letter designation in the following command):

`D:\DCBALL\ASTROLGY\DISK1\SETUP.EXE`

After entering the command, select the "OK" button or simply hit the (ENTER) key to begin the install process.

If you are using Windows 95, installation is as simple as locating the ASTRO SETUP.EXE file on your CD-ROM and double-clicking it.

This is the easy part - the install program will start, automatically creating a directory on your hard disk and will create and install an "ASTRO for Windows" program icon inside the ASTRO for Windows program group box. It will also install a special font called AstGlyphs which allow you to see (both on the monitor and in printouts) the traditional astrological signs or "Glyphs." (Note: During the installation process, you will be asked if you want to install the TrueType or the Adobe Type Manager version of the AstGlyph font. If you have ATM installed, select the ATM version, otherwise, if you don't - or don't know - install the TrueType version of the font.)

Starting ASTRO

The ASTRO install process creates a program group box called "ASTRO for Windows;" locate it and double-click it to open it up.

Here you'll see several icons associated with ASTRO including:

ASTRO for Windows: This is the program icon that you will double-click to start up ASTRO.

ASTRO Help: The online help file which is available anytime ASTRO is run. You may call up ASTRO Help anytime during the operation of ASTRO for details about any part of the program.

ASTRO Documentation: Double-clicking this icon gives access to an excellent 40-plus page ASTRO for Windows Shareware manual which covers all operations and options available to you, including a trouble shooting guide, an astrology dictionary, and an astrological bibliography. (Note: It is *strongly* suggested that you consider printing out this manual as it covers many options and details that are not covered in this book. Besides all that, it's just a darn good example of a complete software operations manual.)

Commercial Use Agreement: This form should be completed and sent to Christopher Noyes if you intend to use the program for commercial purposes.

Registration Form, **README File**, and **VERSIONS File:** Complete one of these forms to register and/or upgrade ASTRO for Windows. Some info about other versions of ASTRO is included in these files.

Let's get started by double-clicking the ASTRO for Windows icon in the program group. You'll see an opening screen (see Illustration 3H) which stays up for a few seconds before you can click it away. Here you'll find copyright information, as well as an announcement that this is the shareware version of the program. Click on the screen to get to the main menu area.

At the main screen for ASTRO, you'll find several menus headings (**File**, **Edit**, **Data**, **Chart**, **Options**, **Utilities**, **Windows**, and **Help**) which give you

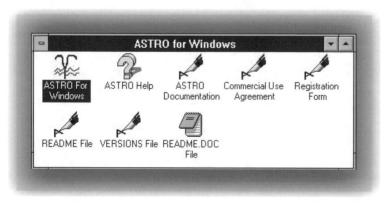

Illustration 3G. Program Group window for the ASTRO for Windows program.

Illustration 3H. The opening screen and shareware notice for ASTRO for Windows.

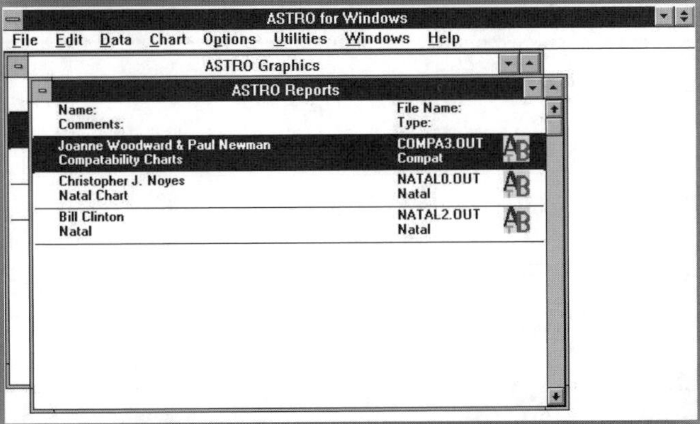

Illustration 3I. ASTRO's main screen with ASTRO Graphic and Report subscreens; note the menu headings.

access to the various features and data entry screens of ASTRO. We'll investigate them as we go along.

You'll also notice two subscreens - ASTRO Graphics and ASTRO Reports - this is where your astrological charts and textual reports will be found once you generate them.

Adding a Person's Birth Information to the database

For now, let's assume that you'd like to create a new birth or Natal Chart for yourself. Begin by pulling down the **Data** Menu and selecting the choice labeled "Birth Info." You will be presented with a rather extensive form window (Illustration 3J) into which you will be entering your birth time and birth location information.

Go ahead and enter your name, sex, birthdate, birth time, and location of birth. You'll do this by selecting the areas of the form you wish to enter information into with your mouse and/or via a series of (TAB) key selections (You can also go in reverse order on the form by selecting (SHIFT) and (TAB) together).

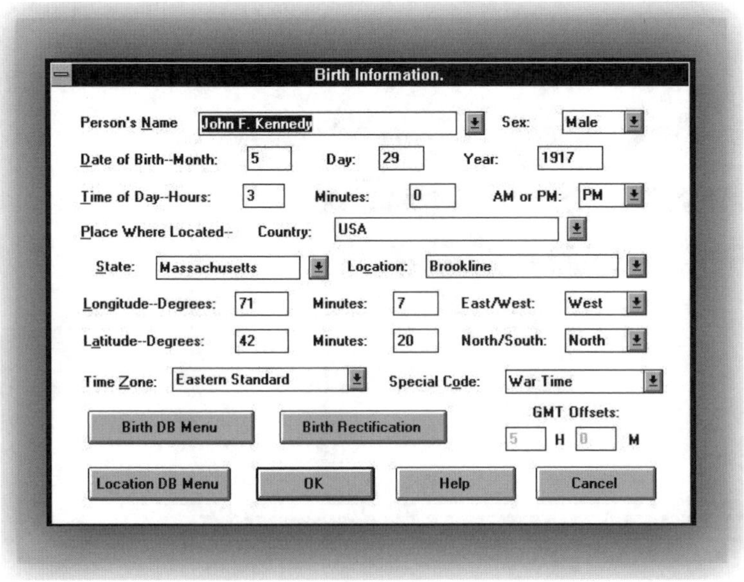

Illustration 3J. Birth Information Screen in ASTRO, where birth and location data is entered.

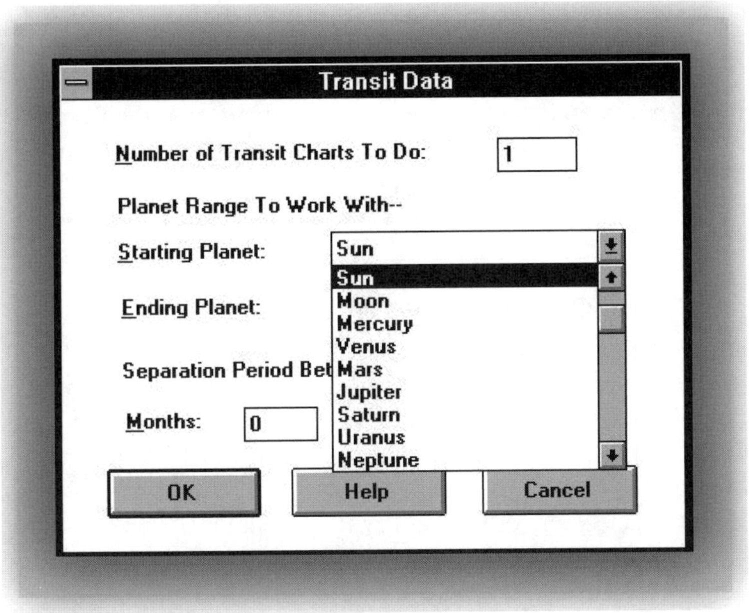

Transit Data

Number of Transit Charts To Do: [1]

Planet Range To Work With--

Starting Planet: | Sun   ▼ |

Ending Planet: | Sun   ▲ |
                     | Moon |
                     | Mercury |
                     | Venus |
Separation Period Bet | Mars |
                     | Jupiter |
Months: [0] | Saturn |
                     | Uranus |
                     | Neptune   ▼ |

[OK]   [Help]   [Cancel]

Illustration 3K. A typical "popup" as found in ASTRO for Windows.

Once entered into the ASTRO birth database, you will not have to re-enter the data each time, but rather you'll be able to call up all the birth information simply by entering the name (or part of it) or by going to the "popup button" (the small button at the right end of the Name field) and selecting it there. Selecting the popup provides you with a quick way of retrieving names that are currently saved in the Birth Database (see the boxed text below for more info on popups). Clicking on one of the names will bring the information associated with that person up into the appropriate fields for ASTRO to work with.

Working with Popups

The popup or "combo" buttons (the buttons located at the ends of the Name, City, State and Location fields) are a quick way to access data already stored in ASTRO's databases. Selecting a popup reveals a scrolling list of selections (names, locations, etc.) that can be selected for easy data retrieval and display. You'll find this feature throughout ASTRO's data entry screens.

To add name or location information to the popup buttons on your ASTRO screen, first enter the data, then save it, (by selecting the "Add a new...to

Database") and then select "Make Popup," either from the screen you are using, or from the selection "Make Popup" under the Utility menu. Once this is done, all the names (and locations) from the databases are updated in the popups. Information stored in the databases will *not* show up in the popups however, until you select the "Make Popup" option - so make sure you perform this function often.

Entering Birth Locations in ASTRO

Working with location information is very similar to working with birthdate and time information. Notice that there are, again, at the end of the Country, State, and Location fields small "popup" buttons. Starting at the Country field, select the popup button to access a scrolling database of countries that are available; scroll down until you find the selection for the U.S.A. (assuming that's where you were born; select any other country if appropriate). This causes the database to limit your choices in the next two fields (State and Location) to allow you to quickly target the city where you were born.

Where's My Hometown?

The shareware version of ASTRO for Windows comes with a database of approximately 200 cities world-wide. Once you register your ASTRO program, you will receive an updated database of over 1200 cities, and an even larger database - more than 30,000 locations - is available from Chris Noyes. This is a good resource should you decided that your calling in life is astrology, and you want to turn pro. Or if you move often.

In the event you do not find your birthplace in the database, you will need to determine the correct latitude and longitude of the location where you were born and enter that information into the ASTRO database. Such information is available from several different locations, including numerous atlases (a good one is the Rand-MacNally Road Atlas). Where else might you check? Encyclopedias have maps and city information; someone at your local municipal airport likely knows the information (one *hopes* Air Traffic Controllers know where they're given directions from), and then there's a source of information that is a virtual goldmine for all sorts of trivial data - your local library. A call to your local librarian will likely provide you with the position location you need (as well as helping you with the mysterious "time zone" issue); don't be shy - that's what they're there for, and most likely they'll be ecstatic to help you out (librarians are like that!).

You can enter in information for your location (if not already available as a popup selection) and store it for future reference by entering in the name of the city with the correct longitude and latitude data, and then selecting the "Location DB Menu" button at the lower left hand portion of the screen. Select "Add a New Location to Database" and then select the "Make Popup" selection from under the Utility menu. Detailed information about the use of "popups" and adding information to databases is included in the extensive ASTRO for Windows Shareware Manual, which is accessed by selecting ASTRO Documentation in the ASTRO Program group. And, at anytime, you can always access the context-driven online help by selecting (F1).

In addition, you'll need to enter in information for the time zone in which you were born which also has popups associated with it. Make sure you have the correct time zone selected for your birthdate, taking into consideration Daylight Savings Time if appropriate (Spring Forward, and Fall Back - and all that jazz).

Once all the birth data is entered and completed, you'll want to save the information to ASTRO's Birth database. You do this by selecting the button at the bottom left of the screen labeled "Birth DB Menu." This brings up another selection window where you will select "Add a New Birth to Database." Also at this time, select "Make Popup."

Birth Rectification

Sometimes you simply don't have all the information that you need about an individual to do a precise birth or natal chart. If you only have approximate birth times (or none at all), this is where Birth Rectification comes in handy. (If you DO have the exact time of birth, Birth Rectification is not needed; simply check the first check box and exit by selecting the "OK" button).

ASTRO allows several ways for dealing with Birth Rectification, depending on how much you know about a person's birth time. A "trial and error" method lets you check a given time against an individual (and their personality profile) to see if it "fits" for them. Interestingly enough, working backwards through the birth rectification process often results in birth times which are accurate within ± 5 minutes! For more details about the particulars of the choices, consult the ASTRO Manual or select (F1) for the help menu.

Compiling Charts Using ASTRO for Windows

Once you've entered in the data for your birth date, birth time, sex, and location - you're ready to start looking at the fruits of your metaphysical labors; that is, you're ready to start looking at some horoscope charts.

You'll notice under the **Chart** menu that you have two choices - "Compile Natal" and "Other Charts." Select "Compile Natal" and you'll see have several different possible charting options, beginning with what is labeled as the "Default" chart. This "Default" chart selection produces probably the most confusing chart of the bunch, and is better off left alone until you've had more time to work with ASTRO, or unless you've already had some experience with astrological charts. Typically, "advanced" astrologers will use this chart selection to produce custom charts. All the details of what appears on the "Default" charts are modifiable by selecting the "Chart Options" under the "**Options**" menu. For more information on what all the details mean, you can select (F1) for Help, or - once again - I refer you to the ASTRO manual which is available by selecting "ASTRO Documentation" in the program group.

For now, let's skip the "Default Chart" (and the next three choices as well) and move right to the "Complete Chart".

Selecting "Complete Chart" will give you the kind of chart that you would normally receive if you were to get one produced by a professional Astrologer - with planetary aspects, birthsigns, houses, etc., as well as an in-depth interpretation of the celestial influences on your life. When you make the "Complete Chart" selection, you'll get a box on your screen that contains the name you entered in the Birth Information window (where you originally entered your name). Selecting "OK" at this point will set the gears of ASTRO in motion to

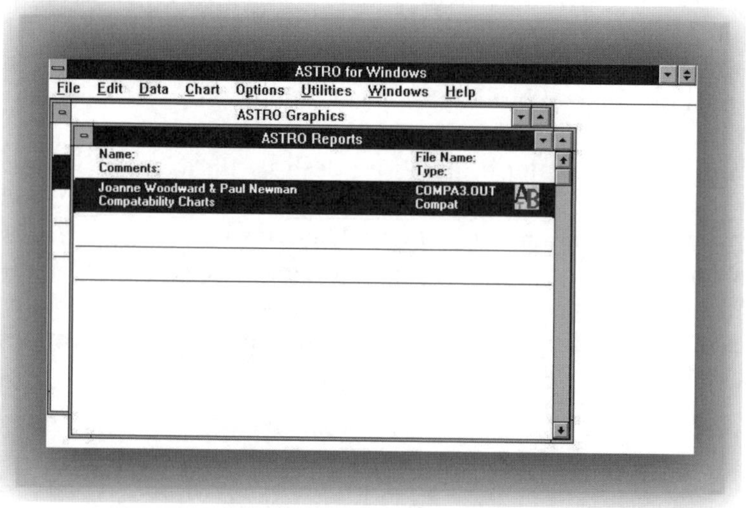

Illustration 3L. The ASTRO Graphics and Report subcreens are where you will find your charts and reports.

start producing the graphic natal chart and textual reports which are at the heart of program.

What occurs - almost instantaneously - is a very complex series of computations of time and space and planetary motions which would take hours or days to compute by hand...so stand in awe for a bit, okay? When this part of the process is complete, you'll have a graphic and textual astrological interpretation which will tell you more about yourself and how you are influenced by the planets than you may even want to know!

Within just a few seconds, you'll find that there are now two new entries on the ASTRO Graphics and ASTRO Reports Screens...with your name on them (Illustration 3L)!

At this point you have the option of selecting either screen by double-clicking your mouse over the new entry area; this will bring up either a circular horoscope chart (if you chose the graphic report, called Natal-Graph), or a textual Report (if you chose the ASTRO Reports selection, simply called Natal). Illustration 3M is an example of a Natal-Graph textual report; 3N is a circular Natal chart.

The textual report is quite lengthy - ten pages or more - and can be either read either the screen or printed out. It's an extensive report listing various astrological details such as what your ascendant is, your planets and their aspects, your house cusps and the signs they're in, your modalities - and much, much more - all with in-depth commentary about what each cosmological nuance means. It's interesting reading to say the least - overwhelmingly so at times.

The graphical chart is the classic circular "cartwheel" horoscope chart which I described earlier in the chapter - with houses, zodiac symbols, glyphs, aspect lines, cusp numbers, and a host of other astrological details available for your viewing. Using the Zoom in/Zoom out features located under the View menu, you can get scroll and view the details of the chart; trust me, there's a LOT of detail to look at.

As I mentioned earlier, ASTRO for Windows is a BIG program, with a lot of hidden features. And there's a LOT of customization that you can do - it's a real "tweaker" paradise. For instance, if you look under the Options menu, you'll find two *different* sets of controls available for customizing the charts you've just produced. Selecting "Graphics Options..." provides you with the opportunity to change the way you look at the "cartwheel" chart. You can change fonts, the colors of every piece of the chart, and there are options for displaying or hiding various components, such as house numbers, "Tick Wheel" options, etc. A separate selection (under "Chart Options") gives you an entirely different set of parameters to manipulate. This same sort of flexibility, in terms of customization, is available for the Textual report as well (choose "Viewer Setup..." under the Options menu to change font size, color, style in the ASTRO Natal Report).

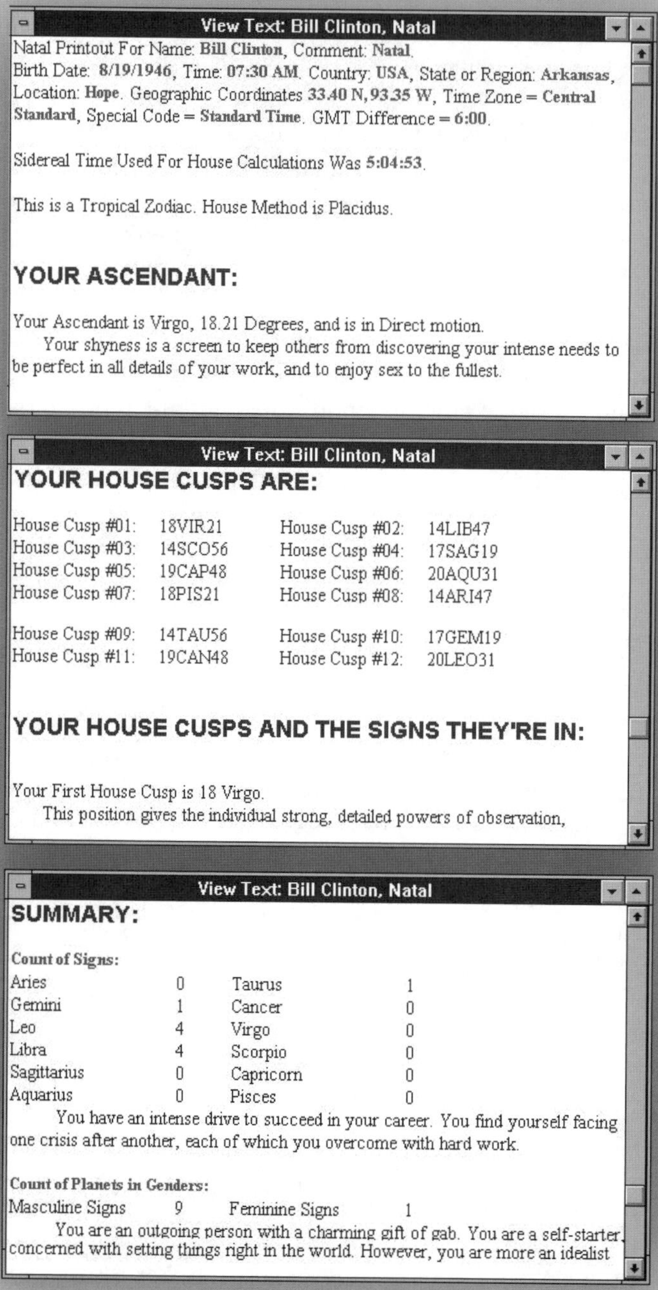

View Text: Bill Clinton, Natal

Natal Printout For Name: **Bill Clinton**, Comment: **Natal**.
Birth Date: **8/19/1946**, Time: **07:30 AM**. Country: **USA**, State or Region: **Arkansas**,
Location: **Hope**. Geographic Coordinates **33.40 N, 93.35 W**, Time Zone = **Central Standard**, Special Code = **Standard Time**. GMT Difference = **6:00**.

Sidereal Time Used For House Calculations Was **5:04:53**.

This is a Tropical Zodiac. House Method is Placidus.

YOUR ASCENDANT:

Your Ascendant is Virgo, 18.21 Degrees, and is in Direct motion.
  Your shyness is a screen to keep others from discovering your intense needs to be perfect in all details of your work, and to enjoy sex to the fullest.

View Text: Bill Clinton, Natal

YOUR HOUSE CUSPS ARE:

House Cusp #01:	18VIR21	House Cusp #02:	14LIB47
House Cusp #03:	14SCO56	House Cusp #04:	17SAG19
House Cusp #05:	19CAP48	House Cusp #06:	20AQU31
House Cusp #07:	18PIS21	House Cusp #08:	14ARI47
House Cusp #09:	14TAU56	House Cusp #10:	17GEM19
House Cusp #11:	19CAN48	House Cusp #12:	20LEO31

YOUR HOUSE CUSPS AND THE SIGNS THEY'RE IN:

Your First House Cusp is 18 Virgo.
  This position gives the individual strong, detailed powers of observation,

View Text: Bill Clinton, Natal

SUMMARY:

Count of Signs:

Aries	0	Taurus	1
Gemini	1	Cancer	0
Leo	4	Virgo	0
Libra	4	Scorpio	0
Sagittarius	0	Capricorn	0
Aquarius	0	Pisces	0

  You have an intense drive to succeed in your career. You find yourself facing one crisis after another, each of which you overcome with hard work.

Count of Planets in Genders:

| Masculine Signs | 9 | Feminine Signs | 1 |

  You are an outgoing person with a charming gift of gab. You are a self-starter, concerned with setting things right in the world. However, you are more an idealist

Illustration 3M.
A small portion of the 10+ page ASTRO Natal report that you can produce.

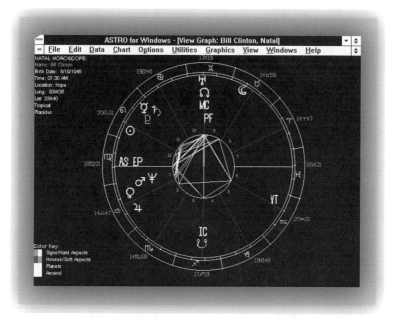

Illustration 3N. ASTRO's circular Natal chart is fully customizable using the Graphic Option features found under the menus.

It would probably take the rest of this book to cover all the details of ASTRO, but let's briefly talk about some of the other major capabilities that are available for you to use.

Transits - Looking into the Future

You can see what ASTRO predicts for your future by entering data into the "Transits Info" screen (found under the **Data** menu). Fill in the necessary data about the first date you wish to analyze (by default, today's date). The "Event of Interest" is you (or any "event" - the start of a new venture, a vacation, a wedding, etc.). Either enter in your name or select it from the popup if it's in the database (and you created a popup). The location information requested here is where you'll be at the time of the transit - not where you were born (unless, of course, you've never strayed from home).

After you've entered the data into Transits Info, select the menu choice immediately below it - "Transits Data" - and fill in the number of periods you want ASTRO to chart for. You can select the time period between each period plotting, but usually you'll just want to choose zero months and one day - to get a daily chart reading.

You'll then need to choose the planets to use in your Transits calculations. It's suggested that you choose the Sun as your first planet and then only go out as far as Venus or Mars, as the outer planets simply don't move a heck of a lot (i.e., their influences don't change much except when the periods between the transit charts is large - months or years).

After you enter the Transits data, compiling the Transits Graphic and Textual Reports is then simply a matter of going to the **Chart** menu, selecting "Other Charts," and then choosing "Transits..." In much the same way as the Natal charts are produced (and ultimately displayed) the Transits charts are available for your review on the ASTRO Graphics and ASTRO Reports Screens.

Compatibility Charts - I Love You Sweetheart, but Our Cusps Need Aligning

Another feature available with ASTRO for Windows is compatibility charting; taking the astrological details of your sweetie and marrying them to your own (so to speak) and seeing where the planets bless (or frown upon) your relationship.

It's a pretty straightforward process to check someone's stars against your own. Under the **Data** menu, select "Birth Info" (the same selection you made to enter in your personal birth date and location info earlier) and make sure YOUR information is showing there. Click "OK" once you verify the information is yours (and not Jimi Hendrix's), then pull down the Data menu once more, this time selecting the "Compatibility Info..." selection, which will give you another birth and location entry form screen, exactly like you completed for yourself - except this time you'll enter birth information about whoever you wish to check out for compatibility.

After you fill in the information for the "simpatico" in question, select "OK" and move over to the **Chart** menu and select "Other Charts," and beneath that "Compatibility..." Once selected you will see a screen which has both of your names (yours and the person you are comparing with); select "OK" and - just as before - the hidden astrological gurus behind the screen get to work - checking out your stars against hers (or his) to see if your ascendants frolic joyfully together across the cosmos...or perhaps that you need to move a few degrees further down the zodiac to search for your astrologically-approved "main squeeze."

Needless to say - you certainly won't get bored with the features and capabilities offered by ASTRO. Explore and have fun with it! It's a full-featured program and by necessity is somewhat complex. There's a lot of depth hidden in the program.

A brief perusal of any complete work on the art and science of astrology will impress you with the details that are included in a complete astrological casting, and ASTRO for Windows does an admirable job of trying to hold true to the tradition. I encourage you to take advantage of the built-in help system (just try (F1) whenever you need some help on a procedure or subject) and do check out the Shareware manual that you can print out to help you navigate the cosmological highways and byways of ASTRO.

Visions for the Macintosh

The Digital Crystal Ball's astrological offering for the Macintosh is a demo version of the Visions program by Lifestyle Software Group. This version has all the same great features as the complete commercial package which includes the ability to create color natal charts that can be viewed on your screen, as well as the ability to provide you with both natal (meaning birth - a "general" profile is provided) and daily horoscope interpretations. The demo version doesn't print or save entries however; therefore you will need to enter in birthdate and location information each time you run the program. A coupon at the back of the book is provided which allows you to purchase the full program, with save and print capabilities enabled, as well as full documentation for Visions.

Visions Information

Visions for the Macintosh is a demonstration version of a commercial program provided to LightSpeed Publishing by Lifestyle Software Group and Nathan Tennies. For details about ordering the full commercial version, please see the order page in the back of this book.

Visions is used daily - by both amateurs and professional astrologers alike - to help produce charts and do interpretations. With Visions' straightforward "no frills" approach and your Macintosh computer, you'll be able to produce - in seconds - natal charts and interpretations that would have taken ancient astrologers weeks to produce. So let's get started...

Starting Visions

You can operate the Visions Demo directly from the CD-ROM if you'd like. Simply locate the Astrology Folder on the CD-ROM and double-click it to open it up. Look for the "Visions Demo" icon and double-click on it to open the Visions program.

Illustration 30. The Opening Screen of the Visions program.

As Visions opens, you'll be greeted by a colorful astrologically-themed wood-cut that includes information about the copyright, and then gives you the names of the original developers - Nathan Tennies, Jeff S. Smith, and Jeff Benegar. A third screen gives information about how to acquire the commercial version of Visions which does include the abilities to print, save, and make new "groups." This same information is seen when you select "About Visions" under the Apple menu.

You may find that you'd prefer to run the program off of your hard disk, for either speed or simply convenience. As with any or all of the programs on the *Digital Crystal Ball* CD-ROM, simply select the Astrology folder with your mouse (click once) and then, holding down the mouse button, drag the folder to the location of your choice, i.e., your hard disk or any other folder you choose. You can even drag the program to a floppy disk, should you wish to share a copy of the Visions Demo with a friend.

Operating Visions - Simplicity Itself

I'd like to say that Visions is a terribly complicated program to operate, but in truth, its simplicity is one of its inherent charms. Once you open the program, there are no complicated forms to complete, no bizarre astrological charts to muddle through - just three simple pulldown menus - **File**, **Edit**, and **Member** - and, of course the ever present **Apple** menu. Let's begin first by looking at what is included under each.

Selecting the "**Apple**" menu under Visions gives you two choices: - "About Visions..." and "Visions Help." Choosing "About Visions..." brings up the colorful copyright screen that appears on startup, while choosing "Visions Help" brings up a small help screen (see Illustration 3P) that gives introductory information about astrology including some history of the science, and then provides an explanation of the components of a natal chart and how it's constructed. Finally, the Help screen discusses the operation of Visions itself. Navigating through the "Vision's Help" menu is a simple matter of selecting one of the seven topics on the right-hand side of the screen and then scrolling through the contents on the left (click the up or down arrows with your mouse to see more of the help information; click the box in the upper left hand corner to close the help feature). If you ever wanted to know what "trisecting the diurnal demi-arc" meant, this is the place to look. (Note: You will find this help window titled "Astrix Help." Astrix was an earlier iteration of the Visions program and apparently the folks at LSG just overlooked it. Not to worry - Help for Visions is complete.)

The next menu selection to the right of the Apple is the **File** menu. Here you find the "Save" and "Print" features which - because this is a demo version - are not accessible to you. Again, a coupon is included at the end of the book to allow you to order the professional version of the program from the publisher - Lifestyle Software Group. The "Quit" command (⌘-Q on your keyboard - see box below for more info) is found here which allows you to exit Visions.

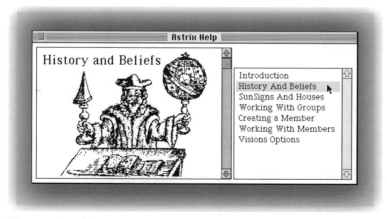

Illustration 3P. The Help Screen from the Visions Program.

Keyboard surfing - Using keyboard equivalents to navigate faster

The key combination "⌘-Q" is a useful shortcut used to quit almost all Macintosh programs. The symbol "⌘" is found on the key (or keys) next to the spacebar on your keyboard (it is also referred to as the "apple key" as it has a small Apple logo on it as well). Like the ⌘-X, ⌘-C, and ⌘-V keyboard commands (which stand for "cut," "copy," and "paste" respectively), ⌘-Q is a command that you might want to commit to memory, as it is keeps down the amount of mouse and menu manipulations that you have to do.

Almost every Macintosh program has keyboard equivalents available. Look for them listed on the right hand side of the menus as you navigate around. Some typical ones you will find are "⌘-S" (for "Save"), "⌘-N"(for "New," as in "create a new file," or as in Visions, "create a New Member"), "⌘-A" ("Select All") and "⌘-Z" ("Undo last command" - good to use when you erase something unintentionally). When you are at the Finder (the top level of the Macintosh desktop) you will find several useful keyboard equivalents listed under the menu selection "Finder Shortcuts."

Under the **Edit** menu, you will find the traditional Cut, Copy, Paste, Select All, and Undo features (again, with keyboard equivalents), and it is also here where you find the "Options..." selection. Choose this selection now to see the options that are listed for Visions.

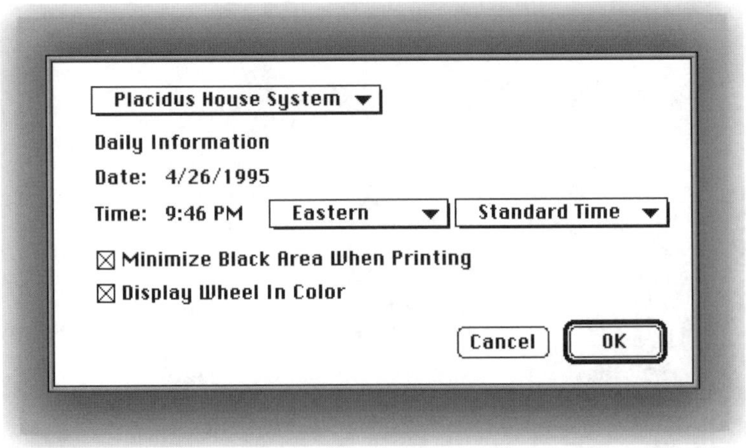

Illustration 3Q. The Options dialog box found in the Visions Demo program.

At the upper left you will find a boxed selection labeled "Placidus House System." By selecting the box with your mouse and holding it down, you will see a "popup" displaying your other "house" choices - "Equal House System" and "Koch System." These are the three most popular charting systems used for the development of natal charts. The differences between them are hotly debated amongst the astrological cognoscenti - the arguments focusing primarily where the actual cusps start in the zodiac. The Koch System was devised by a German astrologer, Dr. Walter Koch, in the early part of this century; the Placidus System was devised in the 17th century by a Spanish Monk named Placidus de Tito, and the Equal House system is the oldest, and remains the system taught by the internationally known Faculty for Astrological Studies in London.

For now, take my word that Placidus is the most common system used for astrological chart development today. I refer you to the bibliography for references that can explain the differences between them; for now, simply allow the "Placidus" selection to remain.

The "Daily Information" beneath the House selection popup gives the current time as indicated by the system clock in your computer. Normally there is no adjustment needed here as it is assumed you want a horoscope for today. However it is possible to cast horoscopes for other days by inputting the date here. By clicking on the date information (month/date/year) you can adjust the date by either keying in a new number or by adjusting the selection using the "up/down" selection feature that will come up. (It's also a good idea to verify that your system clock is accurate.)

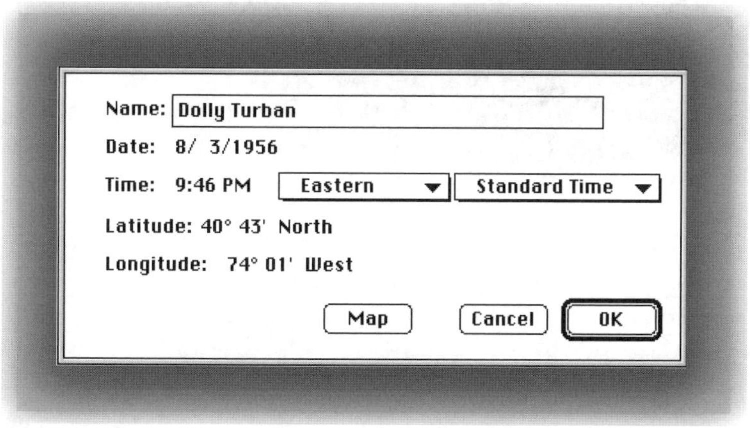

Illustration 3R. Visions' first dialog box for entering in the birthdate and birth time for an individual; note the "Map" selection button.

The two boxes to the right of the "Time" are similar to the House selection popup; choosing them allows you to adjust for the time zone you are in or the one you wish to do a horoscope interpretation for.

The check box "Minimize Black Area When Printing" is not applicable and the second box, "Display Wheel in Color," is normally checked as it deals with display of the Natal charts themselves on your monitor.

The third Menu, **Member**, is where we create a new reading. Selecting "New Member" brings up a dialog box on your screen where we will enter in the information for the person who we wish to develop a chart for; for the sake of example, I have entered the data for Dolly Turban, our fictional online diviner.

Time and date information is entered in much the same manner as in the "Options..." selection shown earlier. You'll note that latitude and longitude for your birth location is requested. This can be entered in manually (like the birthdate and time) or more easily (assuming this information isn't at the tip of your fingers) can be selected using the "Map" button if you were born in the U.S.

Clicking the "Map" button brings up an interactive stylized map of the U.S. (Illustration 3S). Simply enter in the city in question and select "Find City" (a few Canadian cities are also included). If the city is in the Visions database, the appropriate latitude and longitude will be displayed (the proper time zone is selected as well), and a flashing star will appear on the screen at the proper loca-

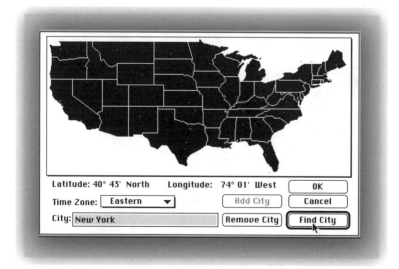

Illustration 3S. Visions' Map selection dialog box where you can enter in the latitude and longitude for your birth location.

tion. If your city is not included though (you'll receive a beep when you try to select "Find City"), simply take the pointer and click on the map where the city is located. The appropriate latitude and longitude will then be displayed on the screen. The "Add City" option is not available to you in the version of Visions included with this book. If you do not know your latitude and longitude, flip back about thirteen pages and see the "Where's My Hometown" box.

Once the proper latitude and longitude have been entered, you then select the "OK" button which returns you to the previous dialog box; there you will note that the latitude and longitude now correspond to those selected on the Map. Click "OK" or select the (ENTER) key to enter in the data into Visions.

At this point you are basically finished entering all the personal data that is necessary. Now you can move on to the next order of business, which is viewing the natal chart and accessing the interpretations that Visions does for you. This is done automatically - and immediately - when you finish entering the personal data by producing a Daily Horoscope chart (See Illustration 3T, which is the window that comes up with the Daily horoscope for the person whose birth data has been entered).

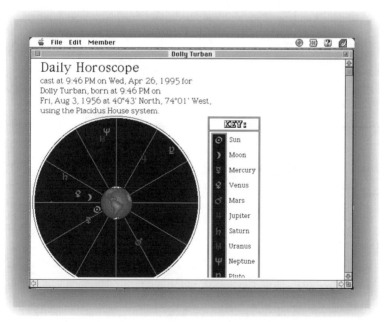

Illustration 3T. This window appears after the proper birth data has been entered. Click on the box in the upper right hand corner to expand to full screen and scroll for more information.

Visions' Charts and Interpretations

By expanding the Daily horoscope window (click in the upper right hand box; clicking in the left hand box closes the window) you can read Visions' interpretation of the influence of the planets on you (we'll assume you have entered your personal birthdate) for that day. Visions takes what it already knows about you from the data you've entered, and compares it to the influence of the rest of the cosmos. Personal issues, career and finance issues, family and friends, conflicts, and romantic concerns are all taken into consideration in an interpretation. Planetary aspects and their influences are discussed, and courses of action are suggested as well.

Under the **Member** menu you will find options which allow you to bring up one of four different kinds of interpretations - a "Natal Horoscope" or "Daily Horoscope," or a "Natal Chart" or "Daily Chart," each of which is topped with the traditional circular horoscope charts at its top. Selecting "Natal Horoscope" and "Daily Horoscope" provides in-depth interpretations of your character and personality, as well as the influences of the planets both in general ("Natal Horoscope"), as well as for the specific day cast ("Daily Horoscope"). The "Natal Horoscope" describes a person's overall personality while the "Daily

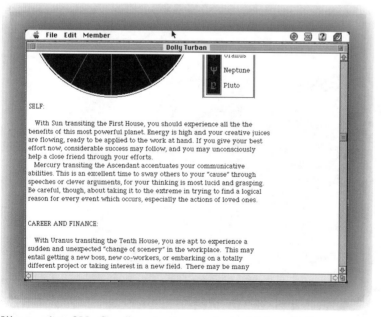

Illustration 3U. Scrolling down reveals the Visions Daily Horoscope interpretation.

Horoscope," as mentioned, provides information about the influences of the planets on the individual at the time the horoscope is cast.

The "Natal Chart" and "Daily Chart" selections provide in-depth textual astrological and astronomical details of the planetary positions, including equatorial declinations, planetary and parallel aspects, house cusps, your ascendant and midheaven signs, your elemental signs, and your modalities. Once again, the difference is that the "Natal Chart" gives a picture of the heavens at your moment of birth, while the "Daily Chart" provides a cosmological snapshot for the moment the horoscope is cast. (Remember, though, that it is possible to do horoscope castings for other times by changing the time frame in the "Option..." selection under the Edit menu.)

The "Group" Concept under Visions and Editing

In the full commercial Visions program, all individuals are stored in what are known as "Groups" (a Group simply being similar folks you group together, such as family members, friends, etc.), but since the Visions Demo only allows you to look at the horoscope of one individual at a time (and you cannot save

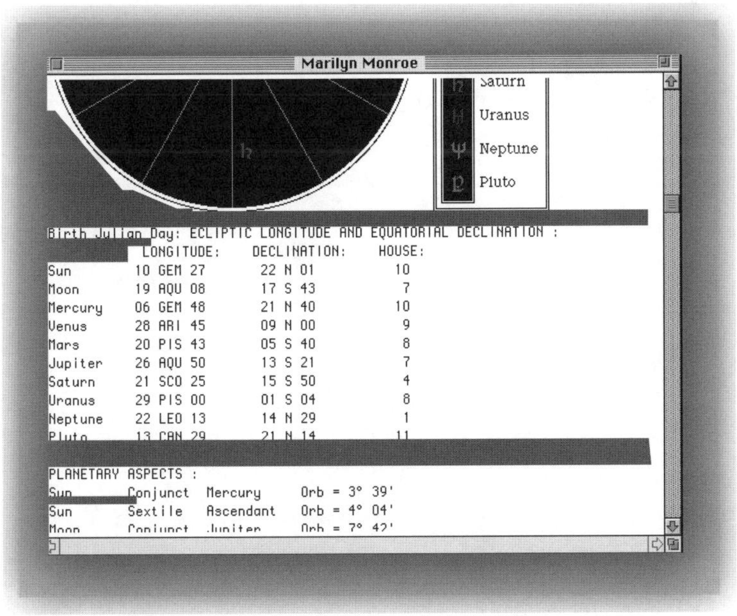

Illustration 3V. Detail from the Visions Natal Chart of Marilyn Monroe showing information on "Eliptical Longitude and Equatorial Declination" and "Planetary Aspects."

the data to the disk), you cannot create new groups. The person's name will appear in a Group box however, after the data is entered. This name can then be selected and edited if need be (using the "Member Info" selection under the "Member" menu). To change birth dates, birth times, or locations of birth, use the same procedures as you used to first enter the name and birth info.

Again, Visions strength is in its simplicity...and its accuracy. In a September 1994 MacWorld Magazine article by David Pogue ("The Mac for Fun and Prophet"), Visions was declared the winner against a group of other divination programs (including a much more extensively-featured and much more expensive astrology program) in terms of its spookily accurate and "riskily specific" predictions....and to think that it does it with just three menus!

The Magic of the Tarot:
Pick A Card, Any Card

Between two worlds life hovers like a star
'Twixt night and morn, upon the horizon's verge.
How little do we know that which we are!
How less what we may be!

-Lord Byron, Don Juan, Canto 15, Stanza 99

History and Overview

If you pick up an ordinary fifty-two card deck of playing cards (yes, the ones with aces, spades, clubs, and diamonds), you'll find the last remaining connection to the traditional Tarot deck - the Fool card in the Tarot's Major Arcana exists today as the Joker.

The question of who originally designed the 78 images of the Tarot, developed the divination rituals, and ultimately determined the meanings for the individual cards, is one that remains shrouded in mystery. The Tarot's imagery and symbology points back in time to numerous cultures, their religions and folklore - to Egypt, India, Babylon, and Tibet - just to name a few. Some say that the true origin of the Tarot is Atlantis, the collective wisdom of that lost continent cleverly encoded into the esoteric and exotic symbols found throughout the Tarot.

Choosing any Tarot card at random and meditating on the imagery there provides some very interesting insights into its influences and origins. For instance, let's look at the Tarot card called "The High Priestess" (card number II). At first glance, it looks simply like some courtly woman between a couple of columns, right? Well, look deeper at the illustration of The High Priestess (Illustration 4A) as we regard the hidden symbols and their accepted meanings.

The woman is the High Priestess herself, seated in the Temple of Solomon between the pillars of Boaz and Jachin - the negative (Black) and positive (White) life forces. On her lap, she protectively holds a scroll inscribed with the

Illustration 4A. The High Priestess (Rider-Waite deck).

Illustration 4B. The Star (Rider-Waite deck).

word "Tora" or Divine Law. The cross on her chest is the solar cross, the upright portion representing the positive male element, and the horizontal - the negative female element (much like the concepts of yang and yin found in the I Ching). Even the decorative tapestry behind her has significance - the palms represent the male force and the pomegranates the female force. On her head is the crown of the full moon, with waxing and waning moons to either side, and a crescent moon at her feet - all symbolic of her position as a "virgin daughter of the moon."

Or choose another Tarot card - The Star (card XVII - Illustration 4B). Here we find a woman pouring water from two pitchers with some stars in the background. Simple enough...or is it? Notice that she's standing with her feet on both the land and the water - and pouring water from the pitchers onto both the pond surface and the bank. Water in this card represents the subconscious, while *terra firma* represents the conscious mind. The seven smaller stars represent the seven chakras of the body, while the five rivulets from the pitcher in the woman's left hand represent the five senses - touch, taste, sight, smell, and hearing. A close inspection of the tree in the background will find a sacred ibis on a branch, representing the thoughts of the mind. (I wonder if he knows where her clothes are?)

The origin of the name "Tarot" is as unclear as the history of the deck itself. In Arabic, there is a word *taraha,* which loosely translated means "to keep out," possibly a reference to the Tarot's "forbidden knowledge." In Hungarian, (Hungary being the traditional birthplace of the gypsy culture, famed for their card reading skills) the word "tar" refers to a deck of cards.

The Tarot is a divination tool that has been in use since at least the 1400's, and probably long before that. The first written reference to the Tarot is found in 1480 in Italy, where its origin was said to be North Africa. Regardless of its origins, with the invention of the printing press, Tarot cards proliferated widely in Europe and eventually in the rest of the world. Recently, there has been a resurgence in interest in Tarot cards, with dozens of decks now available, each with art work and symbology tied to cultures, religions, and concepts as diverse as Native American mysticism and Jungian psychology.

A traditional Tarot deck consists of 78 cards in two sections called the **Major Arcana** and the **Minor Arcana**. The word "Arcana" comes from the same roots as the word "arcane" - meaning secrets.

The Minor Arcana is very similar to a modern-day deck of playing cards in that it consists of four 'suits' (cups, wands, pentacles, and swords) but with one extra card - a Knight - for each suit, bringing the total count to 56 as opposed to 52 (In fact, the similarity between the two types of card decks is so close that it should be no surprise that there is a divination technique that uses regular playing cards called "cartomancy").

The Major Arcana consists of 22 trump cards (The Magician, The Lovers, Death, The Hierophant, Wheel of Fortune, Justice, etc.) each dealing with a major life issue or experience. The Major Arcana cards are sometimes referred to as "keys," and in the context of a reading, the Major Arcana cards are the most important, predicting major events and themes in our lives ("You will soon meet the love of your life").

Allegorically, the Major Arcana can be thought of as representing the stages of a person's life, with the first card - "0" or "Fool" - representing the innocent, naive infant, and its final card - "XXI" or "World" - representing a completion of the learning process of life - in other words, the person becomes "worldly." In the middle we find the "Wheel of Fortune" - but then again, don't we all? (I wonder if Vanna is aware of all this?)

The cards of the Minor Arcana - in contrast - deal more with the mundane day-to-day aspects of living - "You're gonna have a bad hair day today" (not really, but you get the general idea). Each of the four suits is thought to have influence over a particular aspect of a person's life. Although interpretations vary, Wands are generally thought to have influence over the mind and creativity…Cups influence love, happiness, marriage, fertility and sex…Pentacles deal with commerce, wealth, and enterprise (the pentacle looking obviously very coin-like), while the last suit - Swords - deals with the concepts of opposition, strife, courage, and aggression.

Tarot card readings are done in card configurations that are known as **spreads** or **layouts** - the most popular one being the Celtic (sometimes spelled Keltic) Cross. The position of each card in a spread has a particular significance (such as "past influences" or "hopes and fears" - see Illustration 4I later in this chapter). Like poker games, there are many variations of Tarot spreads. Because of its popularity, you can think of the Celtic Cross spread as the Tarot version of "Five-card Stud." The Celtic Cross uses ten cards, some spreads only involve three, some twelve - others involve the entire deck. Many spreads even cross divinational boundaries and take into consideration the influence of astrology and numerology.

Generally a question is posed to the Tarot and meditated upon. Then a card spread is performed, followed by the final step of the process - the "reading" or interpretation of the spread. Using the symbology of the cards, the cards' positions in the spread, knowledge of accepted meanings (and a little intuitive insight), an experienced Tarot card reader can provide information about the querent's future in areas such as love life, career, finances, etc.

In the versions of the Tarot that are included on the CD-ROM (Virtual Tarot for both the Macintosh and for Windows), you'll be able to perform Tarot card readings for yourself and your friends, and have interpretations done for you - all through your computer. Virtual Tarot uses the popular Rider-Waite deck as the basis for its readings (see "The Tale of Pamela Colman Smith").

You'll be able to use the Celtic Cross spread (one of the ten spreads that is available on the commercial version of Virtual Tarot) to perform your own Tarot divination. After posing a question for contemplation, a virtual deck of Tarot cards will be shuffled and presented to you. You'll pick your cards, one by one, and a card spread will be developed right on your screen. After the completion of the spread, you'll simply click on the cards shown on the screen to receive an interpretation of the card and their positional significance.

Interpretations of the Tarot

Like the I Ching, the answers you receive from the Tarot are highly subjective - the allegorical references having meaning to you primarily in the context of your individual life and its events.

In reality the Tarot does nothing. It's simply a collection of images and symbols printed on card stock. In the case of the programs on the CD-ROM, the Tarot appears on your monitor as a collection of electronic dots.

Think of the Tarot as you might a family photo album; the individual photos raise different mental images and impressions for each person who looks at it. Each photo has both emotive as well as factual meaning and impact. The same photo of two people at a beach - a man and a woman - could mean lover, father, sister, happiness (or unhappiness), or any number of other interpretations, depending on the "reader" of the photo, and his or her psychological associations with the image of the photo.

The Tarot is similar - the archetypical images of each card mean something slightly different to each individual who gazes at them, sometimes triggering a meaning or significance at a level more subconscious than conscious - a kind of metaphysical Rorschach inkblot. The Bible, the Jewish Kabbalah, the symbology of the Rosicrucian and Masonic orders, astrology, ancient alchemy, and many other occult, religious, and philosophical traditions have contributed to the rich texture and profoundly deep meanings and messages hidden in the imagery of the Tarot.

The Tale of Pamela Colman Smith

Any one the least bit familiar with the Tarot has probably seen the so-called Rider-Waite version of the deck. It is, in fact, the version of the Tarot that is the basis of the Virtual Tarot program included on your CD-ROM. The Rider-Waite's images and symbols are published in dozens of books on the Tarot, and its world-wide acceptance has made it the deck of choice for most Tarot divination.

With the popular success of the Rider-Waite Deck (more than six million copies of the Rider-Waite deck have been printed...nearly half a billion cards), it is interesting to note that the original artist of the mystical Rider-Waite Tarot images - Pamela Colman Smith - died an obscure pauper.

Born in Middlesex, England in 1878 of American parents, her childhood was spent in London, New York, and Kingston, Jamaica. She graduated in 1897 from the Pratt Institute of Art in Brooklyn, New York and soon afterwards returned to England where she became a theatrical designer and book illustrator.

Around the turn of the century, she joined the Hermetic Order of the Golden Dawn - a secret society whose study of magic, mysticism and human consciousness-raising centered on the traditions of the Rosicrucian order and Occidental yoga. It was there she became associated with the poet William

Butler Yeats (who at one point was the head of the Order of the Golden Dawn), and other notable literary and theatrical luminaries of the time. Besides being an illustrator and designer, she also wrote poetry - no doubt influenced by her famous peers.

After she joined the Golden Dawn, she developed a reputation for her ability to paint mystical visions that came to her under the influence of classical music. In 1909, under the guidance of Arthur Edward Waite (another of the Golden Dawn magician/mystics), she embarked on the task, for token payment, to illustrate the 78 Major and Minor Arcana images - highly allegorical and symbolic in nature - that would ultimately become the Rider-Waite Tarot Deck (the original publishers being William Rider and Son Limited).

Illustration 4C.

If you look carefully at each individual card, somewhere on each is a small, calligraphic artist's signature - the initials PCS. (There is one apparent exception - the Fool, Key "0" - the first Major Arcana trump card. There doesn't seem to be a signature on it...can you find one?)

The Rider-Waite deck is rich in ancient Kabbalistic imagery, and through the design work of Pamela Colman Smith, much of the symbology of the original Tarot was restored, having been lost over time - most likely obscured (or simply eliminated) by artists and printers possibly fearful of the retribution of the Church and its strong stance against all things "occult."

Pamela Colman Smith was never to achieve commercial success in her lifetime, despite favorable reviews of her artwork by art critics, and support by such notables as Alfred Steiglitz, who selected her artwork as the first non-photographic work to be shown at his famous photography gallery on Madison Avenue in New York.

She never married, and died in 1951, all her personal possessions - including much of her life's work - sold at auction to satisfy her debts. It is believed she was buried in an anonymous grave somewhere in Cornwall, England.

Through the Rider-Waite deck however, the mystic vision of Pamela Colman Smith lives on, and touches daily the minds and hearts of the millions of people throughout the world who turn to the Tarot for guidance and direction in their lives.

Maybe - somewhere - the spirit of Pamela Colman Smith looks down and smiles, self-satisfied, in approval that her work lives on as a memorial to her artistry and her efforts to interpret the mystical symbology of the Tarot.

Virtual Tarot (IBM and Macintosh)

Included on your CD-ROM (for both the IBM and Macintosh) in the Tarot category are two folders/directories: the first is a stand-alone version of the Virtual Tarot Celtic Cross spread (excerpted from the full Virtual Tarot program), and the second is a commercial demo of the CD-ROM based Virtual Tarot multimedia program (which also includes access to the Celtic Cross spread). Both are provided to you by Virtual Media Works of Sunnyvale, California.

Program Information

Virtual Tarot for the Macintosh and Windows is a demonstration version of a commercial program prepared especially for LightSpeed Publishing by Virtual Media Works. To order the complete program, see the order page in the back of the book.

Richly-textured and incorporating such experience-enhancing features as full-color 3-D animation, an original music track, video clips, and help and interpretations by voice narrators, Virtual Tarot is an excellent Tarot program. It's a delight to use and experience by both novices and seasoned Tarot readers.

Virtual Tarot is a good case in point when arguing the issue of "hi-tech" versus "high touch" in relationship to performing divinatory activities such as a Tarot reading on a computer. The design of the program actually *enhances* the divinatory experience by incorporating multiple senses (as well as your imagination) into the process.

The designers of Virtual Tarot have taken into consideration the 'total experience' of the querent in the card-reading process and have strived to make the experience of doing a Tarot spread as multi-sensory as possible. Much like a well-designed video arcade game or computer flight simulator, Virtual Tarot lets you "transcend" the traditional human-machine experience and move the experience into another dimension - one of contemplation, and meditative focus. (Another program that accomplishes this same meditation/focus enhancing effect very well is Synchronicity - the I Ching program also included on your CD-ROM.)

Because this is a commercial demo, and not a complete working version of Virtual Tarot, certain features and capabilities have been pared down, or are unavailable to you. The abilities to print and save a reading have been disabled, and of the 10 different card spreads selectable on the full commercial version of Virtual Tarot, you are limited to a Celtic Cross layout.

Even with the reduction in capabilites, you will be able to perform a Celtic Cross Tarot reading with voice interpretations, and you'll have the ability to see and hear the associated Kabbalistic colors and sounds associated with each card.

In the Virtual Tarot demo, you'll also have an opportunity to view (in some detail) images and samples of features available on the full program, including some short video clips discussing the history and philosophy of the Tarot (this capability requires that QuickTime 1.6 or higher be installed in your Mac system folder, or that your IBM or compatible is MPC capable).

Trust me - just because it's labeled "demo" doesn't mean you're going to be disappointed. You will have the ability to do a complete Tarot reading, and I suspect that you'll find that the Virtual Tarot demo alone is worth the price of the book...all the rest of the great programs and information can be viewed as just extra! (See? Your karmic bank account is getting better already!)

A coupon included at the back of the book will let you purchase the full CD-ROM version of Virtual Tarot from Virtual Media Works.

Setting Up to Run Virtual Tarot - Important!

Because of the "multimedia" capabilities inherent in Virtual Tarot, it places demands on your system not normally required by 'main-stream' (i.e. non-multimedia) applications. Because of this, it's important that you set up your computer correctly ahead of time - before attempting to run Virtual Tarot - or you will not be able to take advantage of all the potential benefits, or you may find that the program will not run altogether.

Listed below are minimum requirements for both platforms. There's nothing 'magic' required - no "secret files" or anything. The minimum requirements describe "multimedia-capable" systems which are basically "off the shelf" configurations.

IBM: 386/25 mhz with Windows 3.1, 8-bit (256 colors) monitor with VGA capability, MPC compatible sound card, 4MB (Megabytes) of free application (RAM) memory, a CD-ROM drive, and a mouse.

Macintosh: Macintosh LC or higher, 13" 256-color monitor, 5MB (Megabytes) of free application (RAM) memory - System 7.0.1 or newer, the QuickTime (1.6 or newer) extension, and a CD-ROM drive.

Dealing the Cards...Performing the Virtual Tarot Celtic Cross Spread

IBM: Running the Virtual Tarot Celtic Cross spread on your IBM or compatible is simple - here's how you do it...

First, make sure the *Digital Crystal Ball* CD-ROM is loaded into your player.

Windows 95 users should find the CD-ROM drive in Explorer. Open the CD-ROM by double-clicking. Double-click on the TAROT folder to find a folder called CCROSS. In the CCROSS folder look for a file called CCROSS.EXE. Double-click on that file to run the Celtic Cross spread.

For Windows 3.1 users, from the Windows Program Manager select the "File" menu on the left hand side of the screen, and then choose "Run...". (Assume that your computer recognizes the CD-ROM as drive "D"; otherwise, substitute the correct letter in the following command to designate your drive.)

Into the Command Line box enter in the following command:

```
D:\DCBALL\TAROT\CCROSS\CCROSS.EXE
```

and hit the "OK" button; then sit back and prepare to be entertained and enthralled...the Virtual Tarot Celtic Cross card spread begins.

You can also load the Virtual Tarot Celtic Cross spread from the Windows 3.1 File Manager if you'd like. First make sure the *Digital Crystal Ball* CD-ROM is loaded into your player, then open the "Main" program group on your Program Manager, and then open the File Manager window by double-clicking on the File Manager icon.

Look at the "drive bar" (the top horizontal bar) of the File Manager. Look for an icon that looks like a small CD-ROM being inserted into a drive (most likely labeled "d"). This is the icon which will give you access to the directory of the *Digital Crystal Ball* CD-ROM. Click on it with your mouse to make it the "active" directory (a small box will appear around the icon as shown in Illustration 4E).

Select "Run..." from the File menu and enter the command

```
DCBALL\TAROT\CCROSS\CCROSS.EXE
```

into the "Command Line" of the dialog box which appears. You will then see the Virtual Tarot Celtic Cross spread animation start.

You can also perform the Celtic Cross spread by using the File Manager in another manner. Once you have selected the "d" drive (the CD-ROM drive) on the File Manager's "drive bar," you'll see appear - on the bottom left hand side of the File Manager window - little folders which represent the directories of the CD-ROM; look for one called TAROT and double-click it; an additional folder, labeled CCROSS, will appear beneath the TAROT folder. Make CCROSS the

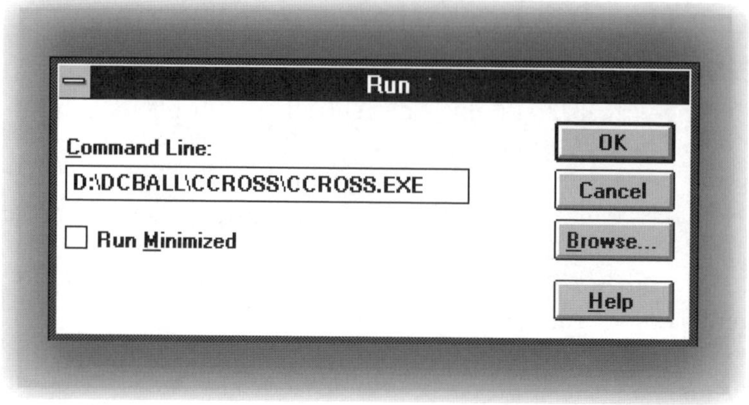

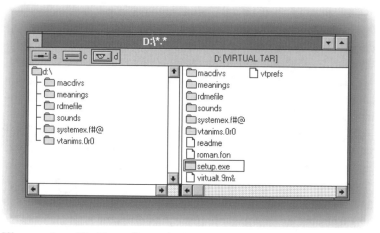

Illustration 4D. To perform the Virtual Tarot Celtic Cross spread from the Windows 3.1 Program Manager, enter this command into the Command Line of the "Run..." selection from under the File menu.

Illustration 4E. To perform the Virtual Tarot Celtic Cross spread from the File Manager, first identify the CD-ROM drive on the "drive bar" as drive "d."

active directory by selecting it with your mouse (again, select the (F5) function key to 'refresh' its contents on your monitor). Look on the right-hand side of the File Manager window now and you will see the contents of the CCROSS directory. Locate a file called CCROSS.EXE and highlight it by selecting it with your mouse, and then either double-click it, or simply select the (RETURN) key. This will begin the Virtual Tarot Celtic Cross spread.

Windows 3.1 Program Group for Virtual Tarot Celtic Cross

The Virtual Tarot Celtic Cross runs under Windows on the IBM and can be installed as a selectable icon on the Windows desktop. Once installed (and with the CD-ROM loaded in the drive), you'll need only to click on the icon on the Window's desktop to run the Celtic Cross layout again.

To put the icon on your desktop, do the following:

1.) Go to the **File** menu on your Program Manager and select "New...", then select "Program Group" and give it the description "Virtual Tarot;" a new program group will be created named "Virtual Tarot," and will appear as an open window within the Program Manager window.

2.) Select **File** once again and "New..."and this time select "Program Item;" a dialog box will appear and into the "Description" type in "Virtual Tarot Celtic Cross." Into the "Command Line" enter:

```
D:\DCBALL\TAROT\CCROSS\CCROSS.EXE
```

Don't select "OK" yet, but rather select the "Change Icons" button. A different dialog box with some icons will appear, but do not select them. Instead, select the "Browse..." button which will bring up yet another box. On the left side of the box, select "CCROSS.ICO" by highlighting it, and then select the "OK" button. Choose "OK" twice more (on the remaining two boxes that will come up) to get back to the Program Manager. You will find that the icon for Virtual Tarot Celtic Cross is now available in your Virtual Tarot program group window. From there, you can then just double click it to run the Celtic Cross layout (assuming, of course, that your *Digital Crystal Ball* CD-ROM is installed in your CD-ROM player).

Macintosh: On the Macintosh, performing the Virtual Tarot Celtic Cross layout is fairly straight-forward, as is running most Macintosh programs.

Simply double-click on the icon on your desktop which represents the *Digital Crystal Ball* CD-ROM, and look inside for a folder called "Tarot" and open it by double-clicking it. Inside that folder you will find two folders - one called "Virtual Tarot Demo" and another labeled "Celtic Cross." Open the "Celtic Cross" folder and look inside for a file called "Virtual Tarot Celtic Cross." Double-click on the Virtual Tarot Celtic Cross icon to begin. We'll discuss the second folder - "Virtual Tarot Demo" - later in the chapter.

Navigating around the Virtual Tarot Celtic Cross...

After you start the Virtual Tarot Celtic Cross (on either platform), both programs are virtually the same. As such, we'll discuss them generically and discuss any differences as they arise.

The meditative music track comes up and the screen dissolves from the black background to a white marble floor which trails off mysteriously, meeting with a star-filled galaxy somewhere in the distance. Columns dissolve onto the screen, a banner reading "Celtic Cross" appears overhead, and the plain white floor transforms into a black and white checkerboard. From the distance, a deck of cards floats in and lands on a ledge (called the "control bar") which rises in the foreground - ready for you to interact with it.

You'll notice that there are several buttons on the control bar. Most are functional, but a few are not (you can, though, hear an audio description of their function by clicking on each of them with the (ALT) or (OPTION) key down). The first button on the left (the one that looks like ◄ ►) is the "Navigation" button and is not functional except in the full Virtual Tarot CD-ROM version of the

Illustration 4F. Here we see Virtual Tarot's interface screen where you will perform the Celtic Cross layout.

program. In addition, the "Interpret" and "Select" buttons are not functional in the demo. The last non-functional button is "Diary" (which appears after you complete the layout and replaces the Select button).

If you click on the far right hand button (the one that looks like a "+"), you'll get a short audio description of the layout of the screen with a description of the functions of the buttons on the control bar, along with directions on how to select the cards from the deck. In the full Virtual Tarot program, this button (and the Navigation button mentioned earlier) are available on most screens to provide easily accessible audio help and navigational aid.

There are actually three ways to exit the Celtic Cross layout. The first is to simply select the most obvious thing on the screen - the "Depart" button. Another way to accomplish the same effect is to click on the Celtic Cross banner across the top of the screen. A third option - ⌘-Q for the Macintosh, or CTRL-Q for the IBM - exits the entire Celtic Cross layout and puts you back at either the Finder (on the Mac) or the Program Manager (if you're using Windows).

One last "hidden" button on the Celtic Cross window is accessed by holding down the OPTION or ALT key, and clicking on the Celtic Cross banner; a brief audio explanation of the Celtic Cross spread or layout will be given. Again, as mentioned earlier, a direct click on the Banner will exit the spread completely.

The Celtic Cross Spread

Alright, now that we're at the proper screen, let's perform the actual Celtic Cross spread.

As you should do with any divination technique, put yourself in a relaxed mode and center your thoughts - concentrating intently (but comfortably) on the issue of inquiry. Maybe it's a question about a love interest (What's the deal with that good looking lady or guy two cubicles over at the office?), a career move (Should I continue to suck up to the idiot I work for, or should I seriously consider that bait and liquor store on the lake?), a financial decision (Put the $2000 in an IRA, or have a heck of a vacation?) - or whatever issue you'd like some input about. Just remember to put the question into clear focus as you click on the deck of cards to choose each of the cards in turn.

With each click on the deck, a card is chosen and placed on the screen in a particular area of the screen - each position has a particular significance (see Illustration 4I). Since the Celtic Cross has ten cards in it, you'll be repeating the card selection process ten times.

An Achille's heel that is often attacked by those individuals who argue that you can't do Tarot readings on a computer (or any divinatory process, for that matter) is the issue of card shuffling, randomness, and the connection between the querent and the process. The complaint is that there is no real "interaction" between the querent and the cards...*Au contraire.*

To quote from the literature included with the Virtual Tarot - "(I)magine a deck of cards on a very quickly spinning "rolodex" inside the computer. When *you* click the deck on the screen, *you* are selecting the next card to be dealt from that electronically spinning deck. If *you* had waited a fraction of a second longer, you would have selected a completely different card." The italics are mine...happier now?

As *you* click on the deck, the cards will appear on the screen one at a time, accompanied by voice narration which explains the significance of the position of the card, as well as an interpretation of the card itself. Also, an associated Kabbalistic tone (that angelic host you hear) and color - different for each card - will come up as each Major Arcana card is dealt. Minor Arcana cards are accompanied only by audio.

In divination, there is the opportunity for a tremendous amount of cross-referencing; the Tarot imagery alludes to aspects of astrology, which in turn relate to aspects of numerology, which in turn refers to the symbology of the Kabbalah, the I Ching, etc. Think of the tones you hear and the colors you see

Illustration 4G. Here you see a typical ten-card Celtic Cross spread as executed by the Virtual Tarot Celtic Cross program.

Major Arcana	Interpretations
0. The Fool	Trust, faith, truth.
I. The Magician	Manifestation, communication, personal power.
II. The High Priestess	Intuition, wisdom, honor.
III. The Empress	Nurturing, abundance, femininity.
IV. The Emperor	Structure, authority, logic.
V. The Hierophant	Teaching, learning, insight.
VI. The Lovers	Making choices, love affair, unconditional love.
VII. The Chariot	Flexibility, momentum, smoothness.
VIII. Strength	Strength, tenacity, courage.
IX. The Hermit	Guidance, help, attainment.
X. Wheel of Fortune	Cycles, change, good luck.
XI. Justice	Fairness, honesty, impartiality.
XII. The Hanged Man	Surrender, transition, sacrifice.
XIII. Death	Transformation, rebirth, death.
XIV. Temperance	Integration, balance, flow.
XV. The Devil	Self-sabotage, addiction, temper.
XVI. The Tower	Collapse, catastrophe, insecurity.
XVII. The Star	Creativity, hopes, health.
XVIII. The Moon	Illusion, dreams, the unconscious.
XIX. The Sun	Success, vitality, cheerfulness.
XX. Judgement	Freedom, potential, letting go.
XXI. The World	Completion, triumph, recognition.

Illustration 4H. The M. L. Foster Interpretations of the Major and Minor Arcana Tarot Cards - Dignified (Upright) [courtesy of M. L. Foster and Virtual Media Works]. Above: The Major Arcana.

Minor Arcana - Wands	Interpretations
Ace of Wands	Beginnings, motivation, inspiration.
II. Wands	Cooperation, partnership, communication.
III. Wands	New path, divine support, travel.
IV. Wands	Harmony, tranquillity, stability.
V. Wands	Strife, struggle, opposition.
VI. Wands	Victory, recognition, awards.
VII. Wands	Capable, courageous, earnest.
VIII. Wands	Rapid acceleration, swiftness.
IX. Wands	Prepared, watching, waiting.
X. Wands	Burdens, responsibilities, oppression.
Page of Wands	Children, bonding, messages.
Knight of Wands	Enthusiastic man, friend.
Queen of Wands	Warmth, enthusiasm, gregariousness.
King of Wands	Enthusiasm, motivation, innovative.

Illustration 4H. *Continued.* The Minor Arcana: Wands.

as resonant frequencies that assist you in calling up the ancestral archetypical imagery hidden deep in your subconscious (sounds like a plausible explanation, doesn't it?). If you don't buy into that theory (there is a lot of literature that does support the concept, by the way), you can select the "Sound" and "Color" buttons and turn off these features - either one, or both. The default position for these features is "on" as indicated by their red color; clicking them will toggle them off or back on. Defeating the color and sound will speed up the process of producing the Celtic Cross layouts considerably. Do not, however, turn off the "Voice" button as this feature is used to give you interpretations of the Celtic Cross spread. (Illustration 4G shows a Virtual Tarot Celtic Cross spread.)

The Celtic Cross demo uses both the Major and Minor Arcana cards (all 78 cards), but shows them only in their upright mode (Virtual Tarot calls this mode "Dignified"; the upside-down mode is referred to as "Ill-Dignified"). Tarot readers and enthusiasts vary on their opinions as to what manner of Tarot

Minor Arcana - Cups	Interpretations
Ace of Cups	New relationships, intuition.
II. Cups	Love, commitment, support.
III. Cups	Fun, socializing, parties.
IV. Cups	Boredom, complacency, closed.
V. Cups	Change, responses, patterns.
VI. Cups	Children, happiness, the past.
VII. Cups	Confusion, choices, options.
VIII. Cups	Leaving, exploring, learning.
IX. Cups	Contentment, pleasure, joy.
X. Cups	Fulfillment, peace, marriage.
Page of Cups	Children, social messages.
Knight of Cups	Nice man, emotions.
Queen of Cups	Nice woman, housewife.
King of Cups	Fatherly, decent, emotions.

Illustration 4H. *Continued.* The Minor Arcana: Cups.

spread (Major Arcana only vs. Major and Minor Arcana, Dignified only vs. Dignified and Ill-Dignified) is the most effective; Oft times the choice depends on the mood of the reader, or the issue being queried.

As the cards are dealt, you will hear two different voices - a male who will give you the card's positional significance, and a female who will provide you with a three-word interpretation of the meaning of the card. The next two charts (Illustration 4H and 4I) can be referred to as you perform the Celtic Cross spread; 4H provides the same interpretations for the Tarot cards as used in the Virtual Tarot demo, and 4I provides a quick reference to the significance of the positions of the Celtic Cross.

As the Celtic Cross layout is being developed, you have the option, at any time, to click immediately on the cards shown to hear again each card's positional significance, as well as the interpretation of the card (along with the asso-

Minor Arcana - Swords	Interpretations
Ace of Swords	New ideas, strong will.
II. Swords	Stalemate, indecision, limitations.
III. Swords	Sorrow, pain, release.
IV. Swords	Rest, alienation, prioritization.
V. Swords	Changing belief systems.
VI. Swords	Improvements, assistance, travel.
VII. Swords	Lack of commitment, partial effort.
VIII. Swords	Self-sabotaging actions.
IX. Swords	Abuse, disturbed, victimized.
X. Swords	Defeat, injury, completion.
Page of Swords	Children, business messages.
Knight of Swords	Action oriented.
Queen of Swords	Intelligent, strong, independent.
King of Swords	Intelligent, strong, leadership.

Illustration 4H. *Continued.* The Minor Arcana: Swords.

ciated color and tone if those features are selected). Also, by selecting the "Reveal" button, you can have the computer deliver a running interpretive audio explanation of the entire spread (or only the portion completed up until that point), again with associated Kabbalistic colors and tones, if so chosen. The "Interpret" feature is unavailable in the demo mode.

Once all ten cards of the layout have been selected and displayed on the screen, you can then 1) select an individual card to hear about it, 2) select the Reveal button to have the narrators provide you a complete audio interpretation of the entire spread, 3) look at the charts I've provided (Illustrations 4H and 4I) and read the meanings there, 4) go fix yourself a nice hot toddy, do your taxes, fertilize your herb garden, call your psychic and set up an appointment

Minor Arcana - Pentacles	Interpretations
Ace of Pentacles	Money, new job, health.
II. Pentacles	Balancing, juggling, travel.
III. Pentacles	Expertise, capability, talent.
IV. Pentacles	Foundations, security, control.
V. Pentacles	Hard times, difficulties, worries.
VI. Pentacles	Money, receiving, sharing.
VII. Pentacles	Restless, uncomfortable.
VIII. Pentacles	Education, training, study.
IX. Pentacles	Satisfaction, environment, comfort.
X. Pentacles	Security, family, prosperity.
Page of Pentacles	Play, security, messages.
Knight of Pentacles	Diligent, practical, healthy.
Queen of Pentacles	Practical, generous, healthy.
King of Pentacles	Finance, abundance, survivor.

Illustration 4H. *Continued.* The Minor Arcana: Pentacles.

for a reading (your therapist, perhaps?), or 5) exit the spread and maybe come back and try the Virtual Tarot Celtic Cross spread again later.

1. Current Conditions - The general "atmosphere" that permeates the question and the various influences at work.

2. Prevailing Energies - Describes what energies are opposing the querent for either good or evil.

3. Basis, or "Root" - The basis or heart of the matter in question.

4. Past Conditions - The influences that are past and fading away.

5. Strong Influences - The immediate and current influences.

6. Immediate Future - Things that will come to pass in the very near future.

7. Apprehensions - This represents the negative feelings of the querent regarding the question.

8. Environment - The influence and opinions of friends and family.

9. Positive Attributes - The querent's hopes and ideals about the situation.

10. Indicated Outcome - This card summarizes the situation and gives an idea of the predicted outcome of the inquiry.

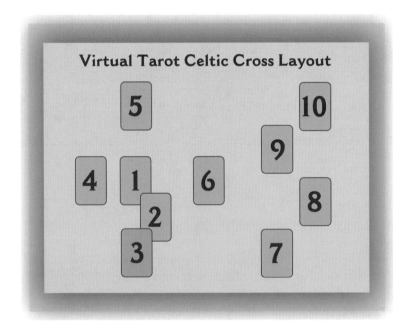

Illustration 41. These are the significances of the positions of the cards in the Celtic Cross layout. As each card is added to the layout, the Tarot comments about your inquiry - from the influences of the "Current Conditions" to the predictions of the "Immediate Future" to the "Indicated Outcome" of the entire issue in question.

A Sample Celtic Cross Layout...Dolly Checks Out Her Career "Oppor-tuna-ties"

Just for grins, let's take a look at what kind of cards Dolly Turban, a lady who, like you, is interested in online divination, conjures up when she uses her mouse to navigate the mysteries of the Tarot.

Dolly's interested in what her current career as a second shift clean-up person in a tuna fish cannery (no dolphins here, mind you) holds for her. Will she rise up the corporate ladder and become a first-shift apprentice packing supervisor? Or will she simply "flounder" at the bottom with the rest of the bottom feeders? Let's see what the Tarot has to say about Dolly's future in seafood!

One of the best ways to interpret a Tarot layout (Celtic Cross or any other layout actually) is to try to view the cards as a running story, pick up on the major themes and general messages being delivered. Don't try to look for exact details, because they're likely to be somewhat shrouded. If you have any true psychic abilities, you may find yourself attuning to the true essence of the querent's question, or the inquiry you are making yourself. Keep in mind that there are two primary components of the layout - the cards' individual meanings, and the specific positions of the cards in the layout.

After formulating the question in her mind, and meditating on it as she selected the ten cards that make up the Celtic Cross layout, Dolly developed the layout as you see in Illustration 4J. The first card she draws is the Devil (card XV). The first card is said to give an indication of the "current conditions." The interpretation of the card is "Self-sabotage, addiction, temper." One way to interpret the first card is that Dolly may be doing something at work to sabotage her advancement, or someone may have some anger about something she's done. Keep in mind that it is generally more important to consider the story as a whole, and not focus on a particular card in a particular position, especially early in a reading, so let's move on and see what comes next.

The second card she chooses - The Lovers (card VI) - represents the "prevailing energies" of the situation which involves "making choices," or a "love affair." Maybe someone in the cannery has an interest in Dolly? Maybe someone in management just "loves" her work!

The third card Dolly draws is the "Basis" or "Root" card, which gives some historical perspective on the question - in this case, the Death card (card XIII). Now, Dolly's goldfish croaked about a week ago (you think there's a cosmic connection there?), but actually the Death card is not generally about death, despite its rather ominous tone and imagery. It's more about change or renewal, especially after destroying old ideas and concepts - in other words, a new start. The interpretation given by the Virtual Tarot is "Transformation, rebirth, and/or

Illustration 4J. Dolly Turban's Celtic Cross layout.

death." A possible interpretation for Dolly is that there's a "change" or "trans-formation" coming in the winds of her career.

Not to belabor the issue, but there's a lot of imagery in the Tarot which deserves meditation upon - the Death card is an excellent example. The immediate interpretation for many people is that the Death card is an evil card, indicating a horrific outcome; all most people see is the skeleton and its associated morbid imagery.

In reality, all Tarot cards have multiple layers of meaning - the true meaning for a particular card's imagery depends upon the skill of the reader and the asso-ciations made in the subconscious of the querent. On the Death card, there are many symbols to be found - both positive and negative in tone. The banner with the five-petalled rose, the two towers in the background with the sun shin-ing between them, the fallen king, the mother and child at the feet of the white horse - all are symbols that tie together and have significance in association to the question being considered. They can even be cross-referenced and linked to similar symbols found on other cards in a given reading. (A very good source book for delving more into the fascinating imagery of the Tarot - as well as the Tarot in general - is *A Complete Guide to the Tarot,* by Eden Gray.)

The fourth card - the Hermit (card IX) - tells us what influences are "passing away" or have been significant in the past. "Guidance, Help and Attainment" are what are passing influences in Dolly's situation. Maybe this is a reference to that conversation Dolly had with her mother where she advised Dolly to give up her dream of being a tuna magnate, and to consider a daytime job in "something with a future," - like telemarketing or envelope stuffing.

The Star (card XVII) is the fifth card of Dolly's Celtic Cross layout representing the "strong influences" at work now for Dolly. "Creativity, hope, and health" are good signs for Dolly, possibly indicative of some clear sailing ahead and maybe a breakthrough in moving towards her goals...she can almost sense that office cubicle with her name emblazoned on the outside in beautiful 48-point Helvetica type.

Card position six is about the "immediate future." Dolly drew the Sun (card XIX), which is an excellent harbinger of success (success, vitality, cheerfulness)!

The Emperor (card IV) in the seventh position deals with Dolly and her "apprehensions" about "Structure, authority, and logic." Will the demands of the position be too great for her? Will she need a cellular phone? Will she have her very own fax machine? Will she (shudder) have to learn how to navigate the Internet?

The "Environment" is the concern of the eighth card - The Moon (card XVIII) - which deals with "Illusion, dreams, the unconscious." Maybe it's all a ruse? Maybe she's reading the signs wrong? Maybe her dream of having her own cannery someday with her at the helm (do canneries have helms?) was all a pipe dream...

"Judgement" (card XX) in the ninth Celtic Cross position deals with "freedom, judgement, letting go." The ninth position deals with "positive attributes." Another way to look at is it represents the querent's hopes and ideals about the subject in question. Dolly again sees the theme of freedom and release - a change in status that might finally allow her to have a date on Friday nights, given that she's been out of circulation for awhile (Dolly's been in charge of the Friday night steam cleaning of the cutting tables at the cannery for the last seven years).

And the last card - the anticipated outcome - is the Chariot (card VII). A marvelous ending card for Dolly, particularly in consideration of the rest of the layout. The literal interpretation is "Flexibility, momentum, smoothness." What's to be interpreted here? Getting this card at the end is very fortuitous for Dolly. According to some Tarot interpretations (such as the classic work on the subject by Eden Gray), the Chariot card means "success, triumph, control over the forces of nature..." In other words, it don't get no better this. We're talking big time success here - a key to the executive washroom, a company Ferrari - and her own personal secretary (male, of course)...skip the cubicle and go directly to the office suite. Maybe all those hours poring over those correspondence courses in Fish cannery waste management will bear some fruit, after all!

Okay, sophomoric humor aside for a moment...I think you get the idea about interpretation. Themes are important in interpreting the Tarot. Sometimes you'll get a reading which seems completely off the mark - what does that mean? Sometimes it means to forget it; come back later and try again when your head is clearer and the issue at hand is easier to concentrate on. Sometimes it's an indication that there's another - perhaps unexpected - event on your horizon. One general suggestion - while it is okay to inquire about the same issue more than once, space the process out some. Asking the same question over and over again will not give good results; wait at least 24 hours before repeating the question. In other words, chill out.

Getting Directly to the Complete Virtual Tarot Demo...

You also have the option of interacting with the complete Virtual Tarot Demo (which also includes the Celtic Cross spread). The Virtual Media Works folks have provided the demo to give you some idea of the contents of the CD-ROM

Illustration 4K. The Opening animation screen of the Virtual Tarot demo.

version of Virtual Tarot, of which the Celtic Cross layout is just one small part. You do this by choosing the other folder/directory included inside the "TAROT" directory or folder on your *Digital Crystal Ball* CD-ROM, and following the procedures outlined below.

IBM: Using the File Manager or Windows Explorer, go to the TAROT directory on the CD-ROM and look inside it for another directory called VTAROT.DIR. Open up that directory and look inside for a file named VTAROT.EXE. Selecting that file (click on it to highlight it) and hitting the RETURN button on your keyboard will bring up the Opening screen of the Virtual Tarot Demo.

Alternately, you can bypass the File Manager routine and choose the "File" menu from the Windows 3.1 Program Manager. Select "Run..." and enter in the command

`D:\DCBALL\TAROT\VTAROT\VTAROT.EXE`

hit "OK" and you're up and running.

Macintosh: On the Macintosh, simply double-click on the icon on your desktop which represents the *Digital Crystal Ball* CD-ROM, and look inside for a folder called "Tarot". Inside that folder you will find another folder labeled

Illustration 4L. The selectable "buttons" - Features, Reviews, and Depart - are located on the bottom of the first interactive entry screen.

111

"Virtual Tarot Demo;" open that folder and double-click on the "Virtual Tarot Demo" icon to begin.

When the Virtual Tarot Demo opens, you will be presented with an opening screen which shows example screens - menus, card spreads, journal entries and other screens - found on the fully running CD-ROM application. If left untouched, the program goes into a "slide-show" mode that dissolves through many of the rich images found on the full CD-ROM version of Virtual Tarot.

At the bottom of the opening screen, you'll find three selectable buttons - "Features," "Reviews," and "Depart." Let's begin with the rightmost button. Selecting the "Depart" button closes the demo and returns you to the Operating System (either the File Manager or Program Manager under Windows, or the Finder Desktop if you are running a Macintosh). Pretty straightforward, huh?

"Reviews" will provide you reviews of the Virtual Tarot CD-ROM from several magazines, including the *Wall Street Journal, CD-ROM World, MacUser, PC Today, Gnosis, Magical Blend,* and others. Selecting any of the magazine titles will give you a excerpt from the magazine reviewing the complete Virtual Tarot CD-ROM program.

Illustration 4M. The "Features" screen allows you to see the capabilities of the Virtual Tarot CD-ROM and also where you can gain access to the Celtic Cross spread.

112

But why trust someone else's opinion when you can delve into and experience Virtual Tarot yourself? Selecting the "Features" button presents you with a list of all the features that are included in the full-blown version of the Virtual Tarot CD-ROM. And it is here also where the Celtic Cross spread (that you performed yourself) is found. Before you select the first feature - "Ten unique & Intriguing card layouts" - click around and investigate the rest of this area for a few minutes by selecting each of the features with your mouse. Animation samples, vocal narrations, and an example of the instructional video clips are found in the Features area.

When you select the 'card layout' feature, you'll see a list of the ten card layouts appear on the right side of the screen (Illustration 4N) along with a "thumbnail" view of each layout (or "spread") at the top right hand portion of the screen. An animation will start and show you each of the spreads in this reduced mode - one after the other beginning with "Calendar" - from the top to the bottom of the list.

When the animation gets to the third spread - "Celtic Cross" - we're treated to a wee bit o' multimedia magic. We are then presented with the same Celtic

Illustration 4N.   Selecting the first feature will bring up a list of Tarot layouts available in the full program and an animation will open the Celtic Cross for you - be patient!

Cross demo that we looked at and operated earlier. See the details discussed earlier for navigating around the Celtic Cross layout screen and for doing a Tarot reading.

Exiting the Virtual Tarot demo is easy. Simply select the "Depart" button on the primary demo screen. If you're in the Celtic Cross layout area of the demo, click on the Celtic Cross banner across the top of the screen. A third option - ⌘-Q for the Macintosh, or CTRL-Q for the IBM - exits the entire Virtual Tarot demo and puts you back at either the Finder (Mac) or the Program Manager (Windows).

Creating a Program Group Icon for the Virtual Tarot Demo (Windows 3.1)

You can also create an icon inside your "Virtual Media Works" program group for the Virtual Tarot Demo by referencing the procedure mentioned earlier in the box titled "Windows Program Group for Virtual Tarot Celtic Cross." Beginning at step two, call the program item "Virtual Tarot Demo", and into the Command line enter the following command:

```
D:\DCBALL\TAROT\VTAROT\VTAROT.EXE
```

Complete the rest of the procedure as written, but select the icon file named VTAROT.ICO instead of CCROSS.ICO. After you complete this procedure, you should have two double-clickable icons in your Virtual Tarot program group - one for the Celtic Cross layout and another for the Virtual Tarot Demo.

With an ever-increasing interest in things such as psychic phenomena, New Age religions, transcendental meditation, and the holistic medical practices and philosophy of the East, it's no wonder that the Tarot - and divination in general - has seen a revival in popularity in recent years. Historically speaking, it seems there has been a cycle of serious use, then disinterest (or even condemnation), then languishing in near-obscurity, and finally, a rebirth of interest in the practices of divination. Such is the case with the Tarot. Today, with the ability to delve into divination practices using software on the home computer (and their associated widespread acceptance), a new and even broader audience has been uncovered - just plain folks like yourself - all practitioners of online divination. Divination...it isn't just for Gypsies anymore!

In the next chapter, we'll look at another divination process that has enjoyed a "rebirth" recently - the Tarot's Eastern divinatory cousin - The I Ching.

5

I Ching:
The Book of Changes and
Your Destiny

Only in quiet waters things mirror themselves undistorted.
Only in a quiet mind is adequate perception of the world.

- Hans Margolius

History and Overview

The I Ching (pronounced "ee" or "yee ching") or "Book of Changes," while typically thought of as simply a tool for divination, is in actuality a classic of Chinese literature and philosophy - one of the six classics of Confucius. Confucius himself was so enthralled by the book's wisdom that it is said he commented once that had he fifty more years in his life to live, he would spend them all contemplating the wisdom of the I Ching.

What is the I Ching? The question is difficult to answer in just a few words...It is both a book of wisdom, as well as a tool for divinatory insight. Its origins are ancient - steeped in the history, culture, and religion of the Chinese.

The book we think of today as the I Ching was heavily influenced by the symbols and issues prevalent during the period of the Mandarin courts. Consulted by the Chinese lords in those Machiavellian-like times, what is today the I Ching has evolved over time, with the following figures as main contributors: the Emperor Fu Hsi, who is thought to have originated the I Ching through the development of the original eight trigrams around 3000 B.C.; Emperor Yu, who promoted the I Ching as a book of wisdom for society around 2200 B. C.; King Wen and his son, the Duke of Chou, (before 1150 B. C.) who contributed the judgements and commentaries on the lines; and Confucius, who added the symbols and his own commentaries around 500 B.C. (although his contributions are believed to be incomplete).

The 64 hexagrams of the I Ching - each of which consists of six lines with associated text - are said to embody the complete wisdom of the Tao, or "the

Way" - an expression of totality and universal law which is the basis of all Taoist philosophy and religion. Simply put, the purpose for consulting the I Ching is to seek guidance in aligning with the Tao. By aligning oneself with the Tao, an individual places him or herself in harmony with the energy flow of the universe. Get out of alignment with the Tao, and you find yourself at odds with the natural order of things. Although it's an overly simplistic analogy, getting out of alignment with the Tao can be thought of as, well, trying to go down a one-way street in the wrong direction - with the resultant consequences.

As a divinatory tool, the use of the I Ching extends back at least three thousand years - and probably further. It originated as an ancient form of Chinese fortune-telling involving the heating of highly-polished tortoise shells and the interpretation of the cracks in the shell which formed as a result.

Given the hassle of gathering and baking tortoise shells (not to mention the stress on the poor turtles), the casting of the I Ching evolved over time to its present methods, involving either a series of coin tosses, a rather complex divination ritual involving the manipulation of 50 thin reeds called "yarrow" sticks (from the milfoil plant), or - most recently - the use of a computer.

No matter what the process used, the end result is to create the characteristic I Ching **hexagrams** (the six-lined symbols) from which the interpretations are made.

Anticipating the invention of binary code (the system of 1's and 0's which is the basis for all computer technology) by thousands of years, the Chinese adopted the I Ching - based on the polar concepts of Yang and Yin - as a model of the machinations of the universe. Both Yang (Masculine, light, positive, active) and Yin (Feminine, darkness, negative, passive) forces were viewed as necessary compliments; every action, thought, force, or object was viewed as a combination of these two opposite forces. All the affairs of men (and the universe) are viewed as fluctuations in the Yang and Yin forces.

In the I Ching, Yang is expressed by a solid, unbroken line:

▬▬▬▬▬▬

and Yin by a broken line:

▬▬▬   ▬▬▬

By combining these lines into groups of three lines called trigrams, the ancient Chinese were able to devise eight symbols which they felt expressed the workings of nature as you'll see in Illustration 5A.

These eight trigrams were then combined - one over the other - to create the 64 hexagrams of the I Ching, which cover 64 situations typically confronted in life.

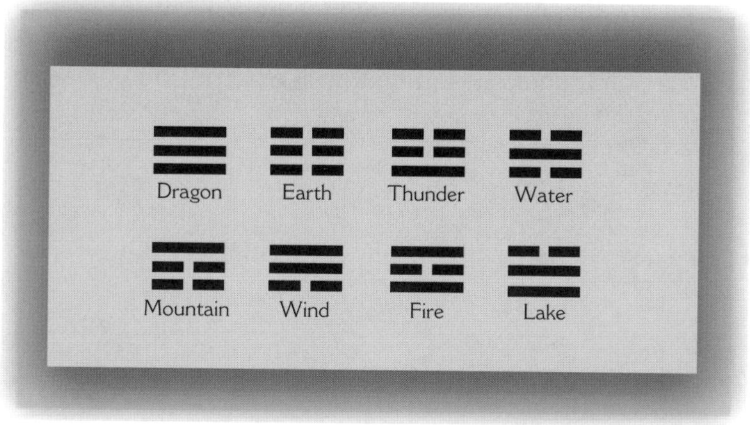

Dragon   Earth   Thunder   Water

Mountain   Wind   Fire   Lake

Illustration 5A. The Eight Trigrams of the I Ching.

Illustration 5B. Hexagram 33, Retreat.

Illustration 5C. Hexagram 26, Strong Potential for Power.

For example, the trigram for Dragon, when placed over the trigram for Mountain, produces the hexagram 33, which is commonly interpreted as "Retreat" or "Withdrawal" - the image is a dragon moving to the top of a mountain in retreat from something. (Illustration 5B.)

By reversing the two trigrams (place the trigram for Mountain over the trigram for Dragon) - you come up with the hexagram 26, interpreted as "Strong Potential for Power" - the image is of a dragon - waiting - gathering power within his mountain lair. (Illustration 5C.)

In these two examples, the dragon can be interpreted as a man (or woman) or a group even - maybe a company or a team. Receiving Hexagram 33 might be interpreted as a call for strategic withdrawal from a situation, whereas, receiving hexagram 26 might be interpreted as assessing a situation and planning before leaping headlong into the fray.

A complete I Ching casting involves the development of a hexagram - one line at a time - from the bottom up. Each of the lines is either fixed or "changing," with the "changing" lines having significant meaning in the particular reading being done.

The I Ching in Your Pocket

Traditionally, the I Ching has been cast by using either a complicated ritual of 'yarrow' stick manipulations or, more commonly, through the tossing of three coins. Bronze Chinese cash coins (with square holes in the center) are a favorite among fortune-tellers in China, and can often be found in flea markets or antiques stores, but you can perform the same hexagram casting by using three coins of any kind - pennies, nickels, dimes, etc.

To generate an I Ching hexagram, we will use the coin's "head" (yang, value 3) and "tail" (yin, value 2) to help us build up a six -line hexagram, one line at a time from the bottom. Simply mix the three coins in your hands and toss them onto a table, and add up the values indicated; the sum of the coins produce a value of 6, 7, 8, or 9, e.g., two heads (3 and 3) and a tail (2) has a value of 8.

The values will give you hexagram lines - both static and changing - as follows:

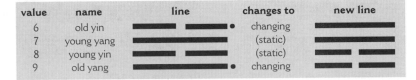

value	name	line	changes to	new line
6	old yin		changing	
7	young yang		(static)	
8	young yin		(static)	
9	old yang		changing	

As each coin toss is completed, a hexagram line is added. After the six lines are completed, look for "changing" lines in your hexagram. If they appear, this means that a second "future" hexagram should be created - built from the bottom up as well - the "changing" lines changing from a split line (old yin) to a solid line (young yang), or reversed - from a solid line (old yang) to a split line (young yin).

Once you have completed both the original ("present") hexagram and the second changed (or "future") hexagram, you can then use the index chart below to determine which of the 64 hexagrams have been created. The top three lines of the hexagram are the "upper trigram"; the bottom three lines are the "lower trigram". At this point, you may reference any complete translation of the I Ching to determine the oracle's advice to your inquiry. Remember the changing lines are referenced in the manner in which they were built up - one to six, from the bottom to the top.

As with the Tarot, and many other divination techniques, the I Ching provides guidance which is generally indirect, highly subjective, and full of allegorical references - often poetic in nature. In fact, many versions of the I Ching are actual rhyming verse in China.

The I Ching program included on the CD-ROM (Synchronicity - for both Macintosh and DOS/IBM) is a complete working demo of the commercial Synchronicity program. This means that some of the utility of the program is reduced or unavailable to you: you can only ask four questions before it transforms into a marketing piece (requiring you to reload a "virgin" copy of the demo), you can only ask one question at a time, and the demo doesn't allow you to print or save a reading. Other than that, it is the same as the commercial version of Synchronicity, including the interpretive display of the I Ching text associated with each hexagram.

LOWER TRIGRAM	UPPER TRIGRAM							
	DRAGON	LAKE	FIRE	THUNDER	WIND/WOOD	WATER/CHASM	MOUNTAIN	EARTH
DRAGON	1	43	14	34	9	5	26	11
LAKE	10	58	38	54	61	60	41	19
FIRE	13	49	30	55	37	63	22	36
THUNDER	25	17	21	51	42	3	27	24
WIND/WOOD	44	28	50	32	57	48	18	46
WATER/CHASM	6	47	64	40	59	29	4	7
MOUNTAIN	33	31	56	62	53	39	52	15
EARTH	12	45	35	16	20	8	23	2

Illustration 5D. Use this Index chart to determine the I Ching hexagram you have created.

Synchronicity requires no complex Yarrow stick manipulations, no repetitive coin tosses - in fact, you don't even have to have a penny to your name. (Well, you do need a Mac or a PC - which can cost a pretty penny!) You just go through a contemplative process involving sitting down at the keyboard, posing a question by typing it into your computer, and then completing a hexagram casting process by holding down some keys on your keyboard, and releasing them when it "feels right." Synchronicity generates the hexagrams for you (with changing lines) and gives you an interpretation of your present situation and the influences acting upon you.

Confucius should have been so lucky... You'll also find two other top-notch I Ching programs included on the CD: Decision Track for the IBM, which focuses on business questions, and I Ching Connexion, which will appeal to the more esoteric minded. Both are discussed later in this chapter.

Anybody know what a Yarrow stick is, by the way? (Doesn't that have something to do with Peter, Paul and Mary?)

Casting the I Ching: Synchronicity (for both Macintosh and IBM)

Synchronicity is the name of the I Ching program included on the CD-ROM for both the IBM and Mac sides of the fence. Because it functions virtually identically on both platforms, we will discuss Synchronicity generically, but we'll point out where there are differences (for instance, when opening the programs).

The program's name, Synchronicity, actually refers to a term coined by the famous Swiss psychiatrist (and contemporary of Sigmund Freud), Dr. Carl Jung. Although the concept is technically more complex than just merely coincidence, the term "synchronicity" basically refers to the phenomenon and significance of coincidence in people's lives.

In 1924, perhaps the most famous translation of the I Ching was written by the German writer Richard Wilhelm; this version was ultimately translated into English by Cary Baynes. In the 1949 foreword of the Wilhelm/Baynes version, Jung (in spite of the scorn and ridicule of his fellow scientists) wrote that he believed that the I Ching was capable of providing penetrating insights into the events and complexities of individuals' lives, and that the I Ching was a perfect example of a cultural phenomenon embodying his "synchronicity" concept. His theory, now commonly echoed by scientists who delve into the murky (but utterly fascinating) waters of quantum physics, basically says that whatever happens in a given moment is tied up with all the other events of the entire universe, at that moment. So, a coin toss is not simply a coin toss, but rather an event that is influenced by everything in the universe - including the subconscious of the individual doing the coin toss.

The demo version of the Synchronicity program included on the CD-ROM is actually modeled algorithmically on the classic yarrow stick method of casting the I Ching. You will be spared the need to do the rather complex yarrow stick manipulation process and will be just dealing with a simple (but effective) keyboard entry process instead.

With Synchronicity, you can use your own computer to access the ancient wisdom of the I Ching. Hexagrams will be cast for you, and interpretations of the hexagrams and their changing lines can be immediately accessed by you from the online database.

A coupon included at the back of the book will allow you to upgrade the Synchronicity demo version included to the full commercial version of the program, which includes a manual and notices of upgrades, etc. The publishers of Synchronicity are promising to have a Windows version out about the time this book is actually released; please contact Synchronicity Software for more information.

Synchronicity Information

Synchronicity for DOS and the Macintosh are shareware demonstration versions of commercial programs by Synchronicity Software. For information about ordering the complete programs, please see the order page on the back of this book.

Opening Synchronicity

IBM: Synchronicity for the IBM is a DOS program. This means that, in order to open Synchronicity on your computer, you will need to create a DOS directory and copy the Synchronicity program files into it. This is a straight-forward process though, so relax and we'll work through this together.

If, after you start your PC, you see a DOS prompt (a DOS prompt looks like C : \ >, as shown in Illustration 5E), you're all set to create a directory and copy the files from the CD-ROM.

If your machine boots directly to Windows however, you'll need to first close down the Windows application to get to DOS. This is accomplished by selecting the leftmost pull-down menu of the Windows screen and moving the cursor down to "Exit." You will then be prompted by, "Are you sure you want to

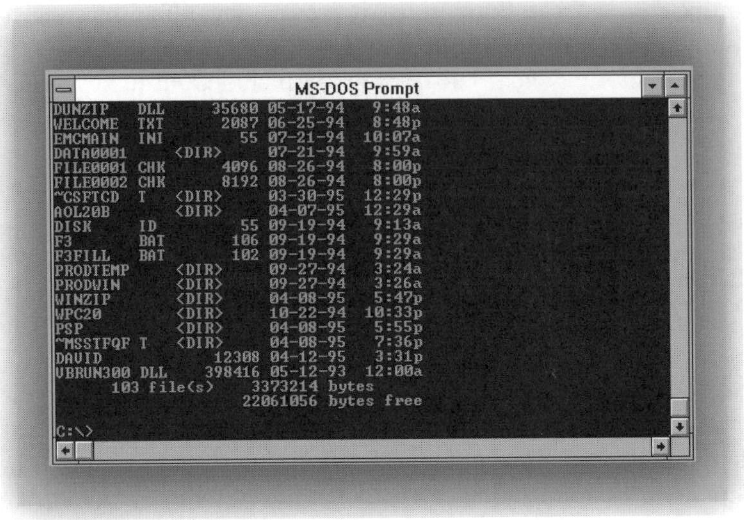

Illustration 5E. The IBM-PC DOS Prompt

end your Windows Session?" Select "Yes" with your mouse or simply hit the
(RETURN) key.

There are two ways to get to DOS from Windows 95. You can press (F8) while
booting your PC, then select "Command Prompt only." Or, in Windows 95
select "Start," then "Programs" then the MS-DOS promt.

Because of the way Synchronicity works on IBMs and compatibles, it is best
to simply exit Windows and run the program from DOS directly. This is
because of the manner in which Windows addresses color on the monitor, and
also because of conflicts caused by memory management utilities used by
Windows.

It is possible to run Synchronicity for IBM under a MS-DOS Prompt while
running Windows, but it involves starting up Windows in a 'limited color'
mode; if you are interested in this, please see the "README" file located in the
SYNC directory on the CD-ROM.

Once you close down Windows, you will be at the traditional text-based MS-
DOS screen shown above in Illustration 5E.

Look for the cursor on the screen next to the "C-prompt". This is where you
will be entering the commands to work with the Synchronicity program.

The Synchronicity program is located on the CD-ROM in a directory called
"SYNC." You cannot run Synchronicity directly from the CD-ROM. You must
first create a directory, also called "SYNC", on your hard disk and copy the files
into it.

124

The order of the process is:

1. Make a directory called "SYNC" on your hard disk.

2. Copy the files from the SYNC directory on the CD-ROM to the SYNC directory of your hard disk.

3. Select the SYNC.EXE file to begin the program.

To do this, follow these steps:

At the DOS prompt (**C : \>**), enter in the following keystrokes exactly as indicated. (We will assume - as we have for all the programs discussed in the book - that your CD-ROM drive is designated as Drive D, and that your hard disk is designated as Drive C; the boldfaced type below is the prompt and the letters and characters after are your keyboard inputs.)

C : \> MD SYNC

Then hit the (RETURN) or (ENTER) key
(this makes a directory called SYNC on your hard disk) Then type:

C : \> CD SYNC

Then hit the (RETURN) or (ENTER) key
(The directory SYNC is selected as the "current" directory on your hard disk)

C : \SYNC> COPY D : \DCBALL\ICHING\SYNC *.*

Then hit the (RETURN) or (ENTER) key
(This copies all files from the SYNC directory on the CD-ROM to the directory on your hard disk)

At this point, you will see the four files be copied - one at a time - from the CD-ROM onto your hard disk. When copying is completed, you will be see the phrase "4 files copied" on your screen and the prompt **C : \SYNC>** will once again return. Then type:

C : \SYNC> SYNC.EXE

Then hit the (RETURN) or (ENTER) key.
(This selects the Synchronicity startup file and loads the program.)

After a few moments, you'll see on your monitor the opening screen for the Synchronicity program. Congratulations, you've successfully opened the Synchronicity program! And you've triumphed over DOS!

Skip over the next paragraph (which explains how to open Synchronicity on the Macintosh) to discover how to use the program.

Illustration 5F. The Opening Screen of Synchronicity for the Macintosh (DOS version is slightly different showing a open pavilion).

Macintosh: To open the program, the first thing you should do is locate the *Digital Crystal Ball* icon on your desktop; this represents your CD-ROM. Double-click on it to open the CD-ROM's directory and look inside for a folder called "I Ching" and open it by double-clicking it. Look inside for a folder called "Synchronicity" and open it. Locate and double-click the icon there called Synchronicity. This will bring up the opening title screen as you see here (Illustration 5F.) Or, if you'd like, copy it to your hard disk by dragging the folder over.

Getting Serene

On both the IBM and the Mac, notice the opening screen and listen to the background sounds. The concept here is serenity - get the picture? The stream gurgles (with "random" frogs in the background) and the image beckons you to leave the stress of the workaday world behind you...enter the frame...and in a meditative manner, calmly contemplate the questions and situations of your life through the use of the ancient I Ching oracle.

From the opening screen, you have a couple of possible choices:

You can simply advance to the next screen by either selecting the (ENTER) or (RETURN) key on your keyboard, or, alternately, you can go to the "Help" area by selecting the "Help" Triangle button (on the Macintosh version) in the lower right area of the screen. In the DOS version, you get to "Help" via the Control-H (sometimes referred to as (CTRL)-(H)) command. Simply press down the (CTRL) and (H) keys at the same time.

Navigating around Synchronicity - On the Mac, the mouse is used to select features. You'll find that it can also be used instead of the (RETURN) or (ENTER) key (click anywhere on the screen) to advance through the screens.

In the DOS version, the mouse is *not* used and all navigation is done via entry on your keyboard.

(A general note - in both the Mac and the IBM version, it is possible to navigate through most of the program simply by hitting just the (RETURN) key. (RETURN) will get you from the opening screen through the intermediate screens, and ultimately will exit you from the program back to either the Macintosh Finder, or the DOS prompt.)

Help Menu

You can get to the Help area at anytime (except during the focusing ritual) by using the (⌘)-(H) key combination on the Macintosh, or (CTRL)-(H) on the IBM.

Selecting Help in either manner brings up the Help menu as shown in Illustration 5G, which is basically a list of key equivalents, which includes:

Quit ((⌘)-(Q) for the Macintosh; (CTRL)-(Q) for the IBM): This shuts the program down and returns you to the operating system (the Macintosh Finder, or back to the "C prompt" on the IBM). Hit this key combination at any time to close the application.

Find a Hexagram by its Number ((⌘)-(F) for the Macintosh; (CTRL)-(F) for the IBM): This brings up a second screen which allows us to choose and view each of the 64 hexagrams of the I Ching and their associated changing lines. Note that this capability is *only* available at the question entry screen.

Make a Demo Copy ((⌘)-(C) for the Macintosh; (CTRL)-(C) for the IBM): Allows you to make a demo copy of the Synchronicity program for a friend (or another for yourself).

Iconize/Expand ((⌘)-(W) for the Macintosh; (CTRL)-(W) for the IBM): Making this selection shrinks the program down on the screen into a small icon. You can get back to the full screen program again by selecting the icon and clicking on it.

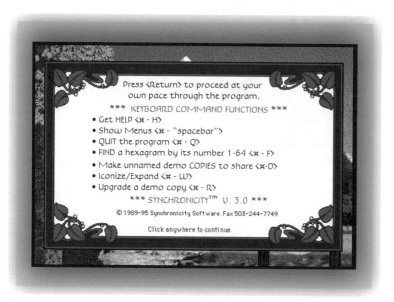

Illustration 5G. The Help Screen as found in Synchronicity (Macintosh version - DOS version is similar).

Upgrade a Demo Copy (⌘-Ⓡ for the Macintosh; Not addressed on the IBM): When you upgrade Synchronicity to a full working program, you can do it through this key combination. A screen comes up for you to enter in registration information.

Not on the Help Menu, but Important

Menubar Option (Macintosh Only): A menubar option is also available by choosing the "⌘-SPACEBAR" key combo. This toggles the menubar on and off; the menubar is normally hidden from view when Synchronicity is running. The menubar offers essentially the same options as mentioned above, as well as a standard file menu (with save feature and printer setup) as well as selections for reviewing past readings, etc. (note: Save and print features are not available in the demo mode)

Sound: The sound level can be adjusted by the use of a keyboard command (⌘-Ⓞ through Ⓝ for the Macintosh; CTRL-Ⓞ through Ⓝ for the IBM), where 0 is no sound, and 9 is the highest volume. This is also documented in another help-type screen which is accessible later in the program. It gives more details about the program and the I Ching's history; we'll look at it in a minute, but for now let's move forward with the actual process of casting the hexagrams.

Illustration 5H. Welcome to Synchronicity.

If you haven't done so yet, let's move to the next screen. Select either the (ENTER) or (RETURN) key, or - if you're using a Macintosh - simply click the mouse anywhere on the screen to get to the Welcome Screen (Illustration 5H).

If you press the (ENTER) or (RETURN) key again (or click the mouse if you're using a Mac), you will go to the next screen which is the "entry" screen for your question or inquiry. (Illustration 5I) Get it? Pen, paper....

In both the Mac and IBM demo versions of Synchronicity, you will be asked to enter your name when you first boot up the application. This personalizes the demo; Synchronicity will inquire if it is you at the keyboard each time you restart for another reading. Any other querent (the term is used to describe the person making the inquiry) is addressed generically as "Friend." When you upgrade to the full version, your copy is personalized and Synchronicity will address you directly by your name, both at the Entry screen, and in the interpretations.

The shareware demo version of Synchronicity allows only four restarts before it disables itself and goes into a "marketing mode." You always have the option of recopying the demo from the CD-ROM, but you can work around this temporarily by using the "Friend" entry when running the demo. We do, however, strongly encourage you to bypass the whole problem by buying the full version of the Synchronicity program.

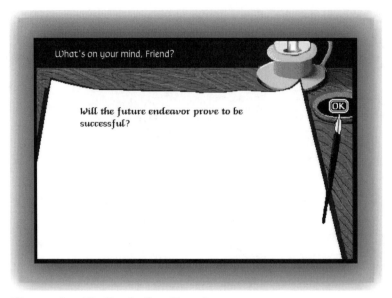

Illustration 51. Ready, Set, Enter!

Posing Questions to the I Ching

The Entry screen is where you write your questions and inquiries to the I Ching. If you are signing on for the first time in the demo mode (or as a friend) you will be presented a short explanation of how to phrase your question; otherwise, you are welcomed by a brief salutatory comment ("May the force be with you", etc.), and then the page is ready for your question to be input.

I Ching inquiries should not be worded as "either/or" or "yes/no" - type questions, but rather should be open-ended inquiries.

A typical I Ching question might be "If I do such and so, what is likely to be the result?" or "What is standing in the way of this or that result?" or, "Would beginning a new relationship with so-and-so be good at this time?" Questions dealing with relationships, health, business, travel, or a myriad of other issues regarding human affairs have been asked of - and responded to - by the I Ching for millenia.

After the question is entered, select the OK button with your mouse (if you have a Mac) or hit the (RETURN) or (ENTER) key. On the Mac version, this brings up a special 'subscreen' on the same page where summary "keywords" can be selected. If your question is ten words or less, then the entire question can be selected; if longer, you may want to either delete some of the words to leave only the important words, or you may want to put in different words than are in the question (this summary subscreen feature is not available on the DOS version). These words will be used in the keyboard "focusing ritual" which follows in a couple of screens.

If you have no specific question, a reading can still be done without entering any words at all on the entry screen. The I Ching will respond with a reading which can be interpreted as a general reading of the state of affairs in your life.

You advance to the next screen by, once again, either selecting the OK button or by hitting the (RETURN) or (ENTER) key.

This and the next two screens (Illustrations 5J) are what you might think of as "focusing" or meditation screens. They don't require input, but rather admonish you to concentrate on your question or inquiry in order to prepare your mind for the hexagram building process. The first of three screens basically suggests you relax; selecting (RETURN) or (ENTER) brings you to the second screen which is a meditative scene with a stream and the candle. You should use time here to get yourself centered and relaxed. Selecting (RETURN) or (ENTER) once again brings you to the last of the three focus/meditation screens which suggests you take another deep breath, and also gives instructions for the development of the hexagram which occurs on the very next screen.

Illustration 5J. After you enter the question, use the three intervening screens (this is the second of three) to meditate on your question and center your thoughts - readying yourself for the hexagram building process to follow.

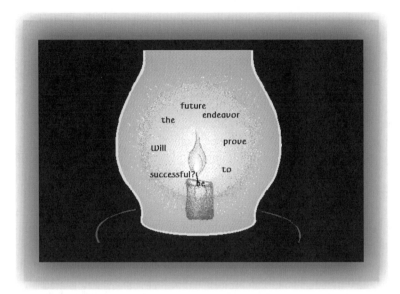

Illustration 5K. On the Macintosh (shown here), you focus on the candle and the keywords spinning around the center. A whirling Starfield beckons you in the IBM version.

Selecting (RETURN) or (ENTER) again brings you to the screen (Illustration 5K) where the hexagrams are built. You'll note the keywords you selected a few screens ago (or the default words - Intuition, Detachment, Clarity, Success) are spinning - slowly - around the center of the screen encircling the flickering candle flame (on the Mac version) or a whirling starfield (on the IBM).

Building your Hexagram

To build your hexagram, simply place your fingers (as many or as few as you like) on any of the keys on the keyboard, and press the keys down, holding them as long as you like. Concentrate on your question. The object is to get the words spinning around the candle flame (or starfield) quickly. When you "feel" like it is the "right time," simply remove your fingers from the keys. A gong will be heard, signifying that the first entry has been accepted into the computer. In both versions, the spinning words will slow down again to the original speed.

This process is repeated twice more to build up the remainder of the six-line hexagram.

There is no right or wrong way to do this; use as many or as few of the keys as you like - the program uses only your timing to develop the hexagrams.

Again, when you feel the time is right, simply lift your fingers from the keys. In this manner, you are intimately aligning yourself and your intuition with the inner machinations of the algorithms of the Synchronicity program (...feel yourself aligning with the Tao?).

When the third key pressing is complete, you will hear the gong again and the words will "spin off" the screen as the scene dissolves to the first page of the interpretation.

Interpreting the Hexagrams

The interpretation screen contains the I Ching's answer to your inquiry. In addition, it has some other features along the bottom, as you'll see in Illustration 5L. (Some of the features are not available to you in the demo versions, but are made available on registration).

On the Macintosh version, the buttons are operated by the use of the mouse - simply click on them to access the feature indicated.

In the IBM version, you will note that beneath each "button", there is an "F-key" (or "function key") designation. The F-keys are physically located along the top of your keyboard and should be pressed to access the particular feature designated.

Illustration 5L. The first page of Synchronicity's interpretations.

At the lower left-hand corner of the screen you will find the six-line hexagram that has been generated as a result of your focusing ritual.

The hexagram on this screen represents the I Ching's response to your question. Notice whether it is composed of only solid (Yang) and broken (Yin) lines. If so, this indicates the hexagram has no "changing lines." This means that the situation described in your inquiry is relatively static and no other information is needed at this time.

If dots are found on the lines of the hexagram, this indicates that the I Ching has also cast "changing lines" and the issue of inquiry is in a dynamic, changing mode. We'll explain more about changing lines in a moment.

For now, let's talk about the rest of the screen. You'll note that at the bottom of the screen - to the right of the hexagram - other iconic buttons appear.

Print: (F1) on the IBM version): *Not available in the demo mode* - The scroll-shaped "print" button allows you to print out the result of your casting, which includes the number of the original or "present" hexagram, the changing lines (if any), and the transformed or "future" hexagram along with the date and question posed.

To the right of Print, you will find either a blank area (if the hexagram cast has no "changing lines") or a button called "Changes."

Illustration 5M. A Changing Hexagram is found at the bottom left hand side of the Synchronicity interpretation screen (Macintosh version).

Changes: (F3) on the IBM version): If this button shows up, it means that the I Ching has added "changing lines" to your reading (you'll see dots on the lines of your hexagram). Changing lines are additional information which add depth and specific meaning to your interpretation and also direct how the original hexagram will be transformed into a second hexagram. The first hexagram represents your "present" situation. The second hexagram is your "future" situation. The changing lines indicate how you will get there.

These changing lines are used to transform the first "present" hexagram into the "future" hexagram by changing solid (Yang) lines into broken (Yin) lines, or vice versa, resulting in a new hexagram.

The interpretive reading at the top of the screen (when you first arrive to this screen) is a comment on the "present" situation; selecting the "Changes" button (if it appears at the bottom) gives you information about the appropriate "changing lines."

The information provided by the changing lines is often the most relevant and significant information you will receive. It is often the changing line information that provides the answer as to what to do in a situation.

After you've reviewed the information in the "Changes" screen, you have only the options to either select the "Present" button (to review the last screen which describes your present situation) or "Next," which takes you to the closing screen and then the exit. The "Future" button - which gives you the I Ching's prediction of the future outcome of your inquiry - is disabled in the demo version of Synchronicity.

The text at the top of the screen is the actual I Ching reading. You'll note scroll arrows on the right side of the screen which you can select to see more of the reading.

Secret - Complete I Ching Text Available in Synchronicity!!

There is a feature which is not generally known (in both the full commercial program, as well as the demo) but of great usefulness. The complete text of the I Ching (with changing lines) is available at the question entry screen (the one with the pen and paper image) by selecting the ⌘-F key combination on the Macintosh, or (CTRL)-(F) on the IBM. This brings up an entry box for you to enter in the number of the hexagram (1 through 64). When you hit (RETURN), the interpretation of that hexagram with line-by-line interpretations for the six changing lines is displayed on the screen.

As mentioned - when using the demo, if you receive a hexagram that contains changing lines, you *cannot* view the future hexagram. However, use the charts provided in this chapter to determine the number of the future hexagram and then restart the Synchronicity demo and get to the "entry" screen (the one where the question is entered). Then use the "Find a Hexagram by its Number" feature (⌘-Ⓕ for the Macintosh; ⒸⓉⓇⓁ-Ⓕ for the IBM) and enter in the number for the future hexagram. You can then read the future hexagram information.

Save: (Ⓕ⑤ on the IBM version): *Not available in the demo mode* - The "Save" feature allows you to save the reading to disk. The information is saved as a standard text file and can be read by any word processing program. The information saved consists of the date, the question asked, and the resultant answer, including the number of the hexagram (the actual graphic hexagram is not saved), its interpretation, and any changing line information as well.

Next: (Ⓕ⑥ on the IBM version): By selecting the "Next" button, you are directed to an additional set of buttons - Ask Again, Readings, Info, Copy, and Exit.

Ask Again: (Ⓕ① on the IBM version): The "Ask Again" feature (not available in the demo mode) allows you to *immediately* return to the original inquiry screen to either ask the same question again, or to pose another question. In the demo mode, you have to exit the program and restart it to ask a new question or to re-ask the last question.

It is okay to ask the same question again of the I Ching or to rephrase your question and re-ask it. Oft times, an I Ching casting will bring to mind slightly different questions or viewpoints on an issue than were originally thought of. Again, this is part of the intrinsic value of the I Ching; it allows you to expand your viewpoint on an issue and to view a situation from a different perspective - perhaps one you'd not considered before.

It is *not* recommended, however, that the same question be asked over and over as this will result in erroneous readings. It appears that oracles have no more tolerance for nagging, pestering questions than us folks on the earthly plane of existence.

Readings: (Ⓕ② on the IBM version): Selecting this button will return you to the last reading that was performed.

Info: (Ⓕ③ on the IBM version): This button brings additional help and general info to the screen. This is similar to the Help screen (⌘-Ⓗ) but gives more info about the nature of the I Ching, Jung's concept of Synchronicity, as well as some helpful hints. (You *can* print out this information by selecting the "Print" button.)

Copy: (CTRL-C on the IBM version): Copy allows you to freely make a fresh demo copy of Synchronicity for a friend to try. The copies you will make are identical to the version you have received on the CD-ROM.

Exit: (⌘-Q on the Macintosh; CTRL-Q on the IBM): This button is selected to close down the application and return to the operating system level of your computer.

What Happened???? My Demo Bit the Dust!

Again - it's a demo, folks...not a complete commercial program. The point of the demo is to give you a program with a lot of utility, but also to encourage you to buy the full commercial version of the program.

On the version of Synchronicity included on the CD-ROM (for both Macintosh and IBM), you can only use a demo version four times, and then it disables itself, turning into a marketing piece. Then there arises a sort of a good news/bad news situation - you *can* run Synchronicity again, but you'll have to create a new demo copy in order to do so (either copy the 'virgin' demo from the CD-ROM or use the Copy feature available on the Synchronicity program itself). To eliminate this problem - go for the commercial program!

Navigating around Synchronicity is pretty straightforward; a couple of passes through the program should have you familiar enough to exercise all the options available in it.

Dolly Checks Out the I Ching - an Example I Ching Hexagram Casting

Dolly Turban - our intrepid online diviner - decided that she wanted to check out the question of balancing her work and romantic life and tap into the wisdom of the Tao hidden in the hexagrams of the I Ching. Undaunted as always, even though she hadn't had a date in months (big time career at the tuna cannery, you understand), Dolly approached the matter with a great deal of seriousness, starting up Synchronicity on her trusty Macintosh PowerBook - intent on seeing what the ancient Eastern oracle had to say about romance in her life...

She had earlier copied the Synchronicity folder (with the program inside) from the CD-ROM on her desktop Mac to a floppy disk to use on her PowerBook. She did this by dragging the Synchronicity folder from the open CD-ROM window onto the icon for the floppy disk that she had inserted into her Mac's disk drive. Those of you with IBMs or compatible portables can copy the Synchronicity directory to a floppy as well, by using Window 3.1's File Manager or Program Manager, or the Windows 95 explorer.

At the entry screen (the one with the pen and paper), Dolly contemplated her inquiry for a few moments, and then carefully entered in her question - "Can I have true love and a career?" She then hit the Return button and - since she had a Mac (you don't have this option on the IBM) - she was presented with the option of editing the question. Since the question was less than 10 words, it wasn't necessary for her to edit, so she opted to move right into the next phase of the Synchronicity hexagram casting process where she was advised to meditate on her question.

She solemnly proceeded through the next three screens (don't be in any rush here; just think about your question) to get to the screen where she would create the hexagram by interacting with the keyboard. In this case (because Dolly is right-brained and uses a Mac) Dolly came to the candle screen with the question, "Can I have true love and a career?" circling the flame.

Dolly concentrated on her question, and then pressed an arbitrary combination of keys on the keyboard - three times - and then released them, allowing the computer, based on Dolly's timing and input, to build up the hexagram which would provide the answer to the question of whether she could balance her love life and her career.

After she had performed the three key pressings, Dolly received an answer to her inquiry, hexagram number 46 - "Pushing Upward". Since there were no changing lines, the reading she received was complete, as follows:

> *Advancement is represented by the forces of growth in springtime, when new plant life pushes upward through the earth's crust. The emphasis is on upward motion, from obscurity to influence, with growth fostered by adaptability and absence of opposition. Constant, flexible growth is the key attribute of a plant pushing upwards. This reading suggests a period of promotion and prosperity in your life.*
>
> *A wise person, in harmony with fate, is sensitive but determined. Make a sincere effort to apply resolute effort against the forces of inertia in life, friend, and good fortune will follow. By remaining tolerant and flexible, you will be able to retain the kind of conscious innocence which fuels growth and advancement. Will power and self-control are necessary to manage this growth properly, but an inner enthusiasm for life is what nurtures it.*

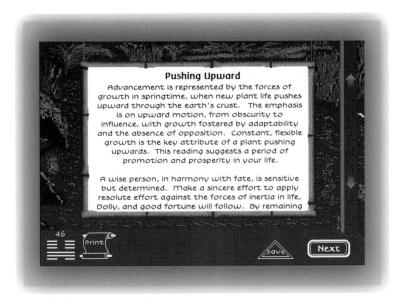

Illustration 5N. Dolly asked the I Ching about balancing her romantic life and her career - and received hexagram 45 - "Pushing Upwards."

So...do you think that Dolly saw this as a positive sign in regards to balancing her love life and her career? "Promotion and prosperity"..."from obscurity to influence"... "Will power and self-control are necessary"...only Dolly really knows what those phrases mean in her own life, but it's pretty safe to say, I think, that the I Ching gave Dolly the "thumb's up" to the issue.

Added Bonus! I Ching Connexion for the Macintosh

For those of you with a Macintosh, we've also included a bonus shareware I Ching program - "I Ching Connexion." This program from the Netherlands is an intriguing and unique application based on the I Ching. We will give you a very limited explanation of its operations (just enough to do a "casting" and interpretation), but we encourage you to delve into the "help" information and the detailed explanation in the menus for more details about the program, its features and operations (...and if you thoroughly figure it out, would you let us know?).

I Ching Connexion Information

I Ching Connexion is a shareware program by Christiaan Freeling and Ed van Zon of Solar Software. If you enjoy using I Ching Connexion, the authors of the program ask that you register—registration information can be found in the Programmer's Note accessible through the program. Note that half of your registration fee will be contributed to UNICEF.

I Ching Connexion is a Macintosh shareware program that offers a *totally* new way of viewing the I Ching, incorporating aspects of "game theory" and a unique hexagram 'visualizing' system that uses interconnecting hexagons, in a special display called a "Connexion." I Ching Connexion also has a complete interpretive text of the I Ching based on the late 19th century "Legge" version of the text.

There are many interesting features built into I Ching Connexion - including a screensaver, a "natal hexagram" caster, and an I Ching "clock" - but the feature of most interest to us (and the one we will describe here) is the casting method which emulates the "three coin" process of developing the hexagrams.

To use the I Ching Connexion to perform a "straight forward" I Ching consultation, open the program and go to the "Oracle" menu and select "Connect." This will cause a screen to appear where - at the top - a question can be entered, and a "Connexion" will appear. (A "Connexion" is a random configuration of the sixty-four I Ching hexagrams. For more information about the significance of the "Connexion," the hexagons, and the I Ching Connexion's particular way of dealing with the I Ching in general, we refer you to the "Help" menu and the information found under the other menus - "Oracle," "Book," and "Connexion.")

Once you've entered in the question, select "Throw the Coins..." from the same "Oracle" menu. Another subscreen will appear where a three-coin tossing process will take place (select the "Complete" button to start the tossing process), and a hexagram will be built - in the traditional bottom to top manner - with changing lines indicated (actually two hexagrams are formed - the left being the "present" and the right being the "future" hexagram). Once the tossing process is completed and the six-line hexagrams are formed, select the "OK" button. Look carefully and you will see a change in the "Connexion." In particular, look for two hexagons - one with a yellow border and another with a light blue border. Inside these hexagons, you will find, respectively, the "present" and "future" hexagrams you have just cast.

Locate the hexagon in the "Connexion" that has a yellow border on it and click on it; this will bring up a textual interpretation of the "present" hexagram.

The "future" hexagram is indicated by a predominant light blue border; click on it to bring up the meaning of the future hexagram (The interpretive text that appears is from the Legge interpretation of the I Ching - the other "major" interpretation being the Wilhelm version).

For a complete explanation of the I Ching Connexion and its various components, as well as the casting and interpretation of the hexagrams, look under the "Help" menu and select "Interpretations."

This is NOT a shallow program, folks - and I'll admit that a good deal of what's said in the text probably goes over most folks' heads (sure did mine anyway - at least in the beginning). But be patient with it. Poke around...see what's hidden...let it grow on you a bit. Like a lot of things in life, you don't have to absorb it all at once. Just take what makes sense at the moment - flow with it - and revisit the program later to partake of a little more, when you are ready.

As an added incentive to register, please note that 50% of the contributions received for the I Ching Connexion will be donated to UNICEF, the United Nations Children's Emergency Fund - a very worthwhile charity indeed.

As your knowledge about the I Ching develops, I think you will find that the I Ching Connexion's breadth and depth - like the concept of the Tao - will make more sense to you.

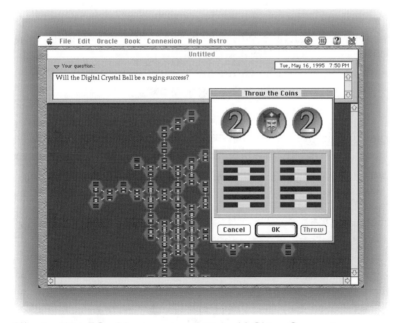

Illustration 50. Here you see a typical I Ching Connexion screen with the result of the coin toss and the "Connexion" in the background.

Added Bonus! Decision Track for Windows

Decision Track is a Windows shareware program from the UK that uses the I Ching to assist in - believe it or not - making tough business decisions. Decision Track is a "lateral thinking tool for decision makers." It supports you in "achieving an intuitive balance between logical thought and emotional *feel* for any situation." Like its bonus cousin - the I Ching Connexion - Decision Track is a *very* full featured program, with the ability to assist you in using the wisdom of the I Ching to make more "informed" decisions - by tapping into your insight and giving you a "second opinion."

Decision Track Information

Decision Track is a shareware program by Tao Management, Ltd. Readers are asked to use the program on a trial basis and, if you enjoy it, you're requested to register your version. Registration information can be found on the opening screen of the program.

Decision Track is a self-installing Windows program that will create its own icon and program group on your Windows desktop. To install Decision Track, go to the Program Manager, pull down the File menu and then select "Run..." Into the Command line, enter in the following command,

```
D:\DCBALL\ICHING\DTRACK\SETUP.EXE
```

and select the "OK" button or hit the (RETURN) key. You'll then see Decision Track's setup window. By default it will look for A:\CHING, but you'll need to change that to:

```
D:\DCBALL\ICHING\DTRACK\CHING
```

Remember if your source disk isn't D: and your destination disk isn't C:, you'll need to change them to the appropriate drive letters.

Decision Track will create a program group called "Windows Applications" and inside, you will find an icon called "Decision Track;" double-click on the icon to open the Decision Track Program.

Windows 95 users need only find the SETUP.EXE file within the DTRACK folder, inside the ICHING folder on the CD-ROM, and double-click on that file.

142

An opening screen giving information about Decision Track (including registration information) will appear; select "OK" to get to the main icon menu.
Here you will see 21 icons across the top of your screen. For an explanation of
each of the icons, select the far right hand icon (it looks like a "+") which will
provide you with the purpose of each icon on the bar.

When you select the "New Problem..." selection under the File menu,
Decision Track goes through a detailed questioning method for dealing with
"business-type" questions. Issues about time-frames, risk, monetary value, etc.
are able to be input as data. However, we will let you discover that aspect of
Decision Track on you own. For now, we will go to the "Quick Decision..."
selection under the File menu instead; here, generalized "one-liner" inquiries
can be posed to the I Ching. (You can also get to the "Quick Decision..." input
screen by selecting the third icon from the left - the one that looks like a small
lightning bolt.)

Type in your question - meditate on it - and then select "OK," or hit the
(RETURN) button. Decision Track will then proceed to create the first (or "current") hexagram and display it on the screen with an associated textual interpretation. It will also show you the Chinese character associated with the
particular hexagram, and the composition of the hexagram (i.e., the name of the
two trigrams that comprise the hexagram). It will also point out (with either an
"x" or an "o") which lines are the "changing" lines. A scrolling screen provides
you with an extensive interpretation of the hexagram shown - again with a slant
or emphasis towards "business" questions.

Information about the meaning of "changing lines" (often the most important part of a I Ching casting) are available by selecting either the "Changing
Lines" selection under the "View" menu, or by selecting the third icon from the
right on the icon menu bar (the one that resembles "barbed wire").

Note that there are two "Yang-Yin" icons on the menu bar - the left one represents the "present" (or "current") hexagram and the right one represents the
"future" hexagram; you can select either to view the associated textual (and
graphic) interpretation of the casting, or - alternately - you can select "Current
Hexagram" or "Future Hexagram" from the "View" menu to access the same
information screen.

Obviously there are a *lot* more selections and features available in both the
menu and the icon bar - you can record your inquiries, schedule alarms, etc.
For more information about the features available, select the icons and bring up
the dialog box or subscreen associated with it - almost every one has a "help"
button available to explain the particular Decision Track feature. Also available
is the general "Help" menu. Also, once you register the program, a "Love I

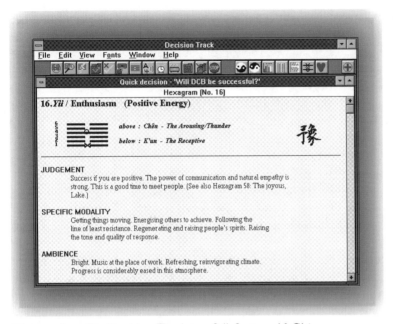

Illustration 4P. Decision Track is a full-featured I Ching program that lets Windows users contemplate the wisdom of the I Ching with complete interpretations, and both hexagrams and Chinese ideograms.

Ching" is made available to you with interpretations with a distinctly "romantic" twist to them (as opposed to the "business" flavor in the shareware version).

Decision Track is a particularly nice I Ching utility program - nicely laid out and navigable; its design shows up well in the manner in which it displays the hexagrams, the associated Chinese ideograms, the trigrams, the changing lines, and allows for easy access to all significant features via the icon bar. And while the interpretations for the hexagrams may not "religiously" follow the Wilhelm or Legge interpretations of the I Ching, they are - without a doubt - the most in-depth (and thought-provoking) that I have seen. Experiment with the features in Decision Track...you'll discover that it's loaded with built-in explanation and Help features, and its operation is very intuitive to boot...and to think that it was a bonus program!

Closing Words

A couple of closing points about using the I Ching in general before we move onto the Numerology programs; first, remember to relax...a clear head and a calm, meditative approach will result in a more accurate casting. This bit of advice is true really for any divination process - not just the I Ching.

Second, you will find that many of the responses you receive will be very accurate - spookily so. This accuracy aspect is one of the main reasons why the I Ching has remained so popular over the centuries.

But many readings will *seem* bizarre or inappropriate for the question or inquiry made. My suggestion is to either expand your thinking and consider the message from a wider perspective, or possibly write down the message and refer to it later. Often an "odd" reading is precognitive - predicting a future event or situation - or it may be a harbinger of an unexpected "turn of events" in the original question you have asked.

There are numerous books available giving more details about the I Ching; at the back of this book you will find several suggested sources for more information - both textual and electronic.

Much wisdom is hidden in the I Ching. For thousands of years, people have relied on the "Book of Changes" for guidance and insight into the events of their lives. Now, through your own computer and the I Ching programs on your *Digital Crystal Ball* CD-ROM, so can you - without even so much as touching a turtle, or having a clue as to what a yarrow stick is!

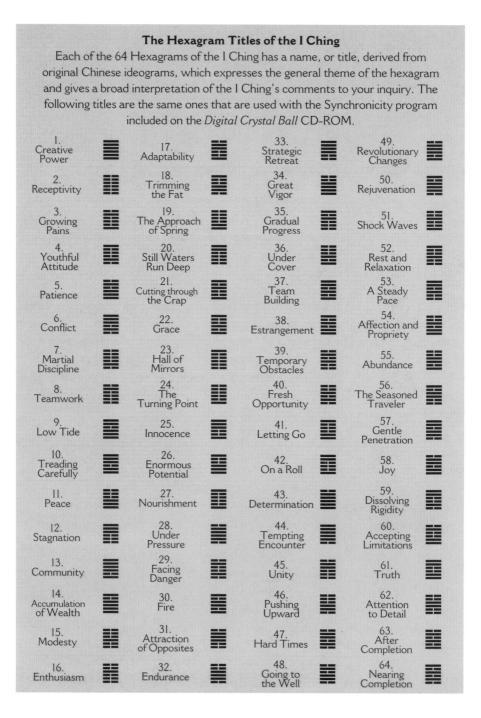

The Hexagram Titles of the I Ching

Each of the 64 Hexagrams of the I Ching has a name, or title, derived from original Chinese ideograms, which expresses the general theme of the hexagram and gives a broad interpretation of the I Ching's comments to your inquiry. The following titles are the same ones that are used with the Synchronicity program included on the *Digital Crystal Ball* CD-ROM.

1. Creative Power	17. Adaptability	33. Strategic Retreat	49. Revolutionary Changes
2. Receptivity	18. Trimming the Fat	34. Great Vigor	50. Rejuvenation
3. Growing Pains	19. The Approach of Spring	35. Gradual Progress	51. Shock Waves
4. Youthful Attitude	20. Still Waters Run Deep	36. Under Cover	52. Rest and Relaxation
5. Patience	21. Cutting through the Crap	37. Team Building	53. A Steady Pace
6. Conflict	22. Grace	38. Estrangement	54. Affection and Propriety
7. Martial Discipline	23. Hall of Mirrors	39. Temporary Obstacles	55. Abundance
8. Teamwork	24. The Turning Point	40. Fresh Opportunity	56. The Seasoned Traveler
9. Low Tide	25. Innocence	41. Letting Go	57. Gentle Penetration
10. Treading Carefully	26. Enormous Potential	42. On a Roll	58. Joy
11. Peace	27. Nourishment	43. Determination	59. Dissolving Rigidity
12. Stagnation	28. Under Pressure	44. Tempting Encounter	60. Accepting Limitations
13. Community	29. Facing Danger	45. Unity	61. Truth
14. Accumulation of Wealth	30. Fire	46. Pushing Upward	62. Attention to Detail
15. Modesty	31. Attraction of Opposites	47. Hard Times	63. After Completion
16. Enthusiasm	32. Endurance	48. Going to the Well	64. Nearing Completion

By The Numbers:
Numerology Tells All

"Evolution is the law of Life. Number is the law of the Universe. Unity is the law of God."

- Pythagoras

History and Overview

Most traditional "mainstream" divination techniques - including those presented in this book - work by providing an all-encompassing paradigm or model for helping a person see how the cosmological "machine" works, and how the gyrations of his or her life fit into the overall scheme of things.

The I Ching accomplishes this through the Taoist-based wisdom of the six-line hexagrams, each of which deals with a major life issue; the Tarot through the imagery of the Major and Minor Arcana and the symbolic hierarchy of royalty, soldiers, priests (and priestesses) and common people; and Astrology seeks to explain the ups and downs of life through the all-pervasive influence of heavenly bodies over the personality and destiny of the individual.

By seeking answers and guidance through one or more of the divination techniques, the querent is provided with a metaphorical window, so to speak, through which he can view his or her own life within a larger framework - as a link in the machinations of the world, and ultimately, the universe. So, in a very real sense, divination can be thought of as a means for tapping into the wisdom of a higher consciousness, or as a way of viewing your life within the larger "divine" order of things. As the saying goes - one man's magic is often another man's religion...

Each system assumes there is an order in the events of people, and in the universe as a whole - precise, even mathematical in its nature. From the microcosm of the atom, to the macrocosmic interactions of the planets, mathematically precise associations abound. Nowhere, though, is the significance of numbers more central - or more important - than in the study of the science of Numerology.

Numbers are found everywhere in divination - the 64 hexagrams, the 78 cards of the Major and Minor Arcanas, the 10 planets and 12 sun signs of the Zodiac - each has a special meaning and significance in the particular cosmology presented by the I Ching, the Tarot, and Astrology.

Pythagoras - the Greek mathematician, philosopher and mystic - is commonly credited as being the father of modern Numerology, having believed to have been taught as a young man the numerical mysteries of the Kabbalah. Famous primarily for his formula (remember the formula for calculating the lengths of the sides of a right triangle?), Pythagoras saw the entire universe ultimately reducible to numbers. And he also felt that numbers had special vibrational energies which represented spiritual existence. Pythagoras felt that everything in the universe ultimately operated in predictable progressive cycles.

The Bible is full of numbers; a quick perusal of the Book of Revelations or Ezekiel provides a literal feast of numerical references - the number of the Beast or 666, the 144,000 chosen ones, the seven seals, etc. Many academicians and theologians believe that the numerical references in Revelations have their origins in Numerology (perhaps linked to the esoteric wisdom of the Kabbalah), and it is only through a knowledge of the meaning of the numbers themselves that the true meaning of the strange symbology of the Biblical references can be truly understood.

The practice of Numerology essentially involves taking certain alphanumeric aspects of your life (your name, your birthdate, your address, etc.) and "reducing" them into **personal numbers** - the "Life Lesson Number," the "Path of Destiny Number," the "Soul Number," the "Personality Number," the "Karma Number," the "Survival Number," etc. These numbers all deal with your growth and development on this plane of existence, and ultimately, paying back the National Bank of Karma. The names of the various numbers derived differ depending upon the reduction technique referenced (or the software program used). And some reduction methods (such as the one used by "Prime" in the Macintosh section) incorporate the numbers of the birth time, as well as the name and birthdate; still others might incorporate your address or other pertinent alphanumerical information.

In essence, the reduction (or delineation) process involves, for example, taking your name, and applying numerical values to the letters - a is 1, b is 2, c is 3, and so forth. When we get to letters represented by double digits (J being 10, W being 23, etc.), we "reduce" these to single digits by adding the individual digits together to come to a single number (W is 23; we add 2 and 3 together

1	2	3	4	5	6	7	8	9
A	B	C	D	E	F	G	H	I
J	K	L	M	N	O	P	Q	R
S	T	U	V	W	X	Y	Z	

Illustration 6A. This chart provides easy translation of alphabet characters into their numerological equivalents for "personal number" derivation.

to get 5). This process of reduction to a single numerical value is the cornerstone process of numerology. Illustration 6A is a chart of the numerological values of the letters of the alphabet reduced using this method. Even very large values can be ultimately reduced to a single digit in this manner.

There are various formulas used for the delineation process, depending on the particular "school" of numerology adopted, but generally the process involves the derivation of - at a minimum - four primary personal numbers .

The first (usually called the "Soul Number") is derived by adding together all the vowels of your name. The Soul Number generally refers to the "inner you"- the essential personality that is hidden from the public, but which shows up in your closest relationships. Also it addresses what - at a deep level - motivates you to action. (The question of whether or not the letters "y" or "w" should be treated as vowels or consonants is debated by professional numerologists, but seems to be largely an issue of personal choice.)

The second personal number is found by adding together the numerical value of all the consonants (this gives what is generally referred to as the "Personality" number). This is your "external image" - the image displayed to the public and the overall persona that you project.

The third is found by adding together *all* the letters - consonants and vowels (this gives the "Path of Destiny" number). This number refers to your life "mission" and what you are to accomplish and achieve in this lifetime.

And the last of the four major numerological numbers - The "Life Lesson" number - is derived from "reducing" your birthdate. Sometimes called the "Karmic Lesson" number or "Missing" number, this number refers to the personality traits and characteristics that you need to develop in this lifetime.

In addition, some methods produce more than just four primary personal numbers (i.e., Prime produces five - the "Survival" number actually is a reduction of the combination of the Birth and Destiny numbers).

As an example, My "current" name (Guy D. Smith, the name I usually use) ultimately reduces as follows:

The vowels reduce to 1:

Name	G	U	Y	D	S	M	I	T	H
Vowel Count		3	7				9		

3+7+9= 19; then 1+9 = 10; then 1+0 =1. So my Soul Number is 1; I have assumed that "y" is a vowel.

According to one source, a Soul Number of 1 is interpreted as meaning that - among other things - my desire for independence and independent thinking is my prime motivation. I am cautioned to look at this strong drive and not to let it get in the way of achieving the practical goals of life, including satisfactory personal relationships. In reality, this is a fair assessment, as I have always viewed myself as an "independent thinker" - often to my own detriment (stubborn little cuss that I am).

In numerology, you'll often find multi-digit numbers expressed in the form "15/16" or "43/7"- the number after the slash mark being the reduced value of the multi-digit number found in front of the slash mark. In the example just mentioned, my Soul Number would be expressed as 10/1. Often the "secondary number" - the multi-digit number - has special significance and is used by the professional numerologist doing the actual delineation. For example, the numbers 11 and 22 are *not* reduced further, but are referred to as one of the "Master" numbers which deal with major accomplishments and traits of "genius;" persons who have these numbers pop up in their delineations are believed to have special skills as artists or future leaders.

The consonants in my name reduce to 8:

Name	G	U	Y	D	S	M	I	T	H
Consonant Count	7			4	1	4		2	8

7+4+1+4+2+8 = 26; then 2+6 = 8; So my **Personality Number** is 8 (or 26/8). A Personality Number of Eight supposedly represents people who are independent, persuasive and, generally speaking, in control. It is recommended that I should always appear well-dressed and present a successful-appearing personality. (Hmmm...perhaps I really *should* clean out some of those old moth-eaten suits from my closet...maybe shine my shoes more often.)

152

My full name (consonants and vowels) reduces down to 9:

Name	G	U	Y	D	S	M	I	T	H
Full Name Count	7	3	7	4	1	4	9	2	8

7+3+7+4+1+4+9+2+8 = 45; then 45 is ultimately reduced to 9 (4+5); So my **Path of Destiny Number** is 9 (or 45/9). Supposedly perfection is the goal of the individual with a 9 Path of Destiny Number, with many tests and setbacks (that reminds me, I need to file my taxes), but ultimately learning forgiveness will bring temperance (with the IRS?).

As mentioned earlier, your Life Lesson Number is derived from your birthdate. For example, if your birthdate is October 19, 1953 (okay, I admit it...it's mine), then your Life Lesson Number is calculated as follows:

First, write the date out in the format 10-19-1953 (use the full year, not 53), and then add the numbers together and reduce them as you did with the names:

Birth Date	1	0	1	9	1	9	5	3
Date Count	1	0	1	9	1	9	5	3

1+0+1+9+1+9+5+3=29; then 2+9 = 11; so my **Life Lesson Number** is 11. Remember, you don't reduce 11 down further because it's a "master" number. Hmm....I wonder if that master number 11 means I should pursue the Great American Novel? Or maybe the Great American CD-ROM?! Actually it seems - more than anything - to suggest that I have a need to develop a sense of altruism and community, and to strive for balance between my material, physical, and spiritual lives.

The same basic process can be used on addresses, company names, pet names, locations, and so forth, to derive different numerologically significant numbers.

Obviously, this whole reduction process can get a little tedious...adding together all the numbers in a name like Dorothy Elizabeth McGillicutty-Smythe is an exercise in patience, to say the least. A slip in the math and you might have old Dory accountable for tons of undeserved Karmic debt!

But never fear - the computer is here! Put away the paper, pencils, and calculator. With the numerology tools on the CD-ROM (*Prime* for the Macintosh and *Personal Numerologist* and *Intimacy* for the IBM), you'll be able to give Lady

Magillicutty-Smythe her personal numbers almost as quickly as you can key in her name.

You'll also get an interpretation of the values *and* you'll be able to see how your numbers and someone else's (friend, foe, spouse, lover, boss) link up (or not). Just remember, it's all in fun.

Now, if you *misspell* the name...

And by the way, A-squared plus B-squared equals C-squared...

The Kabbalah

The Kabbalah (there are many variations on the spelling) is an ancient body of Judaic esoteric mysticism which has strong influences on the Tarot, Astrology and Numerology. The word "Kabballah" itself means "to receive;" tradition says that the Kabbalah was originally given to Moses by the angel Gabriel, and was passed down orally from teacher to pupil. Written references to the Kabbalah first appear during the Medieval period following the dispersion of the Jews into Spain, Africa, Italy and throughout the rest of Europe.

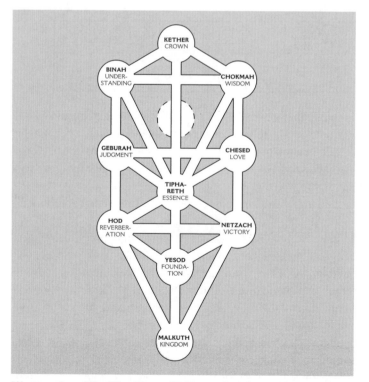

Illustration 6B. The Tree of Life symbol from the Kabbalah.

Through its Tree of Life symbol, the Kabbalah offers a model of the universe and the creation process embodied in a symbol involving ten interlinking spheres - beginning on the earthly plane, progressing upward through eight other planes, and culminating ultimately at the top sphere, which represents the unity of the universe.

Each sphere (called a Sephiroth) is connected to the other spheres by connecting links or "paths," twenty-two in number. Twenty-two is a recurring number in the field of divination and corresponds to many different things - there are 22 letters in the Hebrew alphabet, there are 22 cards in the Major Arcana of the Tarot, and the number 22 is a very important number in Numerology, being one of the "master numbers."

Numerology Programs

For Numerology Divination, we offer two related programs for IBM and compatible PCs, and a Macintosh program.

Intimacy and Personal Numerologist for the IBM PC

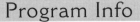

Program Info

Personal Numerologist and Intimacy are made available to you on a 60-day, free, trial basis, courtesy of Widening Horizons. If after this period of time you decide you like these programs and continue to use them, Widening Horizons asks that you pay a registration fee. Registered users will receive more up-to-date releases that contain important features missing in the trial versions. Refer to the exit screens for more information. Though the registered versions of Personal Numerologist and Intimacy do not include the right to sell the reports, Widening Horizons does offer a professional series of numerology programs that do give you this right. See their ad in the back of the book.

The numerology programs included on the CD-ROM for the IBM are called Personal Numerologist and Intimacy - both shareware programs published by

Widening Horizons software (specialists in numerology software) of Woodinville, Washington. Both programs are designed to run under DOS and were originally developed by Matthew Goodwin, author of *Numerology: The Complete Guide*. We've provided both programs, as they each have a slightly different purpose. Personal Numerologist provides you with a tool for looking at the numerological profiles of individuals - yourself, friends, lovers, bosses, co-workers, or anyone else who may be significant in your life. Intimacy provides you with a means of delving into the numerological influences at work in your romantic interests, allowing you to look at the forces and issues that exist between you and another person.

Both Personal Numerologist and Intimacy are DOS programs and require that you copy their directories to your hard disk in order to run them, but both are relatively small programs (Personal Numerologist and Intimacy each take up approximately 600k - about 1.2 megabytes for both). They are complimentary, but either (or both) can be put on your hard disk (or on a floppy if you prefer), and run separately from the other.

Copying the Numerology Programs to your Hard Disk

DOS: Since these are DOS programs, they can be copied in a number of ways: from DOS, from Windows 3.1, or from Windows 95.

We recommend you copy files through Windows, but if you prefer DOS, then make sure you are at the C-prompt, as explained in Chapter 2. If your CD-ROM drive is labeled D and the disk you want to copy to is C, then type the following command at the C-prompt:

```
C:\> COPY D:DCBALL\NUMRLOGY\PERSNUM
```

This will copy the Personal Numerologist directory from the CD to your internal hard drive. To copy the Intimacy program, substitute INTIMACY for PERSNUM in the Copy command.

Windows 95: If you are using Windows 95, find the "PERSNUM" folder in the "NUMRLOGY" folder on the CD-ROM using either My Computer or Windows Explorer. Click on the "PERSNUM" folder, open the "Edit" menu and click "Copy," open your C disk, and then click "Paste" on the "Edit" menu. Alternately, you can simply drag the "PERSNUM" folder from the CD-ROM to your destination disk (making sure the destination disk is visible), and it will be copied.

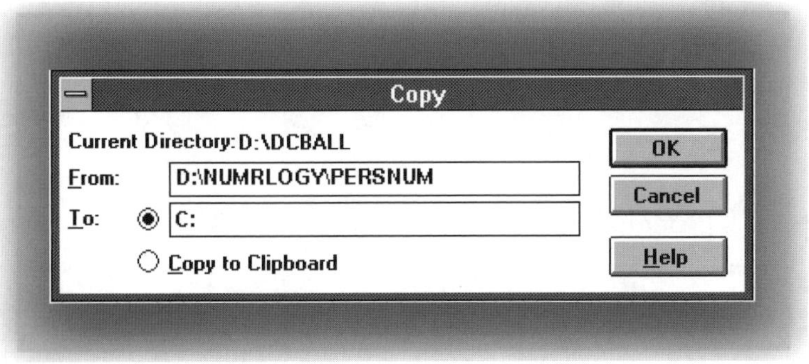

Illustration 6C. The dialog box that comes up under "Copy" at the Windows 3.1 File Manager. Enter in the command exactly as shown to copy Personal Numerologist.

To copy the Intimacy program, click on the "INTIMACY" folder instead of the "PERSNUM" folder.

Windows 3.1: The first thing you need to do to copy (and ultimately open) Personal Numerologist is to get to the File Manager (we'll discuss Intimacy in a few moments). Once at the File Manager, click on the "File" menu option to open the pull-down menu (the leftmost menu at the top of the window). Under "File" you will look for and select "Copy...", which will bring up a dialog box asking for information as shown in Illustration 6C.

Use your keyboard to enter in - exactly as shown - the following command:

`D:\DCBALL\NUMRLOGY\PERSNUM`

This will direct your computer to search on the CD-ROM (here designated with the letter "D") for a directory called PERSNUM and to copy it with all of its contents to your internal hard disk - usually named "C" (you may substitute the CD-ROM drive designation letter "D" for any other letter, should your particular configuration be labeled differently - i.e., "E" or "F", etc.).

You may also copy Personal Numerologist to a floppy disk if you'd prefer; just insert a formatted floppy disk into your floppy disk drive and substitute the letter "A" for the letter "C" in the command line above (this assumes that your floppy drive is designated as "A"; if it is designated with a different letter, use that letter in the command line instead).

To copy the other program Intimacy to your hard disk, we use a very similar command at the "Copy..." command line entry screen,

`D:\DCBALL\NUMRLOGY\INTIMACY`

This command will copy the Intimacy directory with its associated files onto your hard disk. All the same information regarding CD-ROM and hard disk naming conventions, as well as the option of copying the program to a floppy disk, applies here.

Opening "Personal Numerologist" and "Intimacy"

Both programs - once you've entered in the data requested and asked for the programs to calculate the delineations - allow you to view the produced report either on your computer screen, or as a printed report.

We'll start out by opening up and operating "Personal Numerologist" in some detail; both programs operate very similarly and once you've learned how to operate and enter data into Personal Numerologist, Intimacy should be a snap to use.

Windows 95 and DOS: You'll want to get to the DOS C-prompt in either Windows 95 or DOS. See Chapter 2 for DOS instructions. In Windows 95, choose "MS-DOS Prompt" from the window labeled "Programs."

At the C-prompt type:

```
C:\PERSNUM\PN.EXE
```

See the operating Instructions in the following Windows 3.1 section.

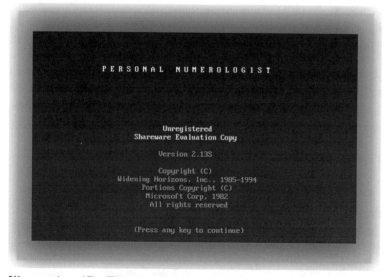

Illustration 6D. The opening screen for Personal Numerologist with copyright notice and shareware information.

Illustration 6E. The first selection screen of Personal Numerologist. From this screen, you may access an in-depth help file or proceed to the first personal data entry screen.

Windows 3.1: At the Windows 3.1 Program Manager, choose the "Run" selection from the "File" menu which will bring up the dialog box. Into the command line, carefully enter in the following command (this assumes you have correctly copied the directory from the CD-ROM to your hard disk as described earlier):

`C:\PERSNUM\PN.EXE`

Within a few moments, the familiar Windows desktop will disappear and a DOS window will open for "Personal Numerologist" as shown in Illustration 6D; this screen contains copyright information, and information about Personal Numerologist, including a notice that this program is shareware.

We strongly encourage you to consider the advantages of registering *all* of your shareware programs and remind you that often, it is only through the shareware distribution method that many excellent programs - such as Personal Numerologist - get distributed.

Select any key on the keyboard to get to the first selection screen (Illustration 6E). Here you have the option of either going to the first entry screen by choosing the default "N" (do this by pressing the (RETURN) or (ENTER) key), or to view the online "Help" information (by entering a "Y" from your keyboard and then selecting (RETURN) or (ENTER)).

Getting Help in Personal Numerologist

Choosing "Y" here will bring up an extensive help listing which gives you an online overview of the features of Personal Numerologist (see Illustration 6F), as well as the details of entering information into the various prompt screens that are presented to you as you progress through the program. Specific help for each screen is also available as you operate the program by selecting the (F1) function key found at the top of your keyboard.

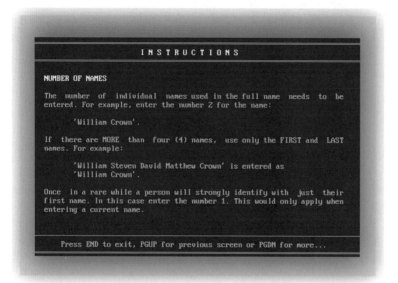

```
┌─────────────────────────────────────────────────────────────┐
│                    I N S T R U C T I O N S                    │
├─────────────────────────────────────────────────────────────┤
│ NUMBER OF NAMES                                               │
│                                                               │
│ The  number  of  individual  names used in the full name  needs  to  be │
│ entered. For example, enter the number 2 for the name:       │
│                                                               │
│       'William Crown'.                                        │
│                                                               │
│ If  there are MORE  than  four (4) names,  use only the FIRST and  LAST │
│ names. For example:                                          │
│                                                               │
│       'William Steven David Matthew Crown' is entered as      │
│       'William Crown'.                                        │
│                                                               │
│ Once  in a rare while a person will strongly identify with  just  their │
│ first name. In this case enter the number 1. This would only apply when │
│ entering a current name.                                      │
│                                                               │
├─────────────────────────────────────────────────────────────┤
│      Press END to exit, PGUP for previous screen or PGDN for more... │
└─────────────────────────────────────────────────────────────┘
```

Illustration 6F. Typical screen from the Help file of Personal Numerologist, here giving information about entering in the number of names.

If you select "Y", you'll receive information about the following topics:

- **General Information** about Personal Numerologist.

- **Number of Names** information, i.e., if your name has more (or less) than two names.

- **Name Entry**, including how to deal with your name if you are adopted, the difference between Birth Names and Current Names, and hyphenated names.

- **Birth Dates**.

- **Editing** your entered information.

- **Function Keys** and their use in Personal Numerologist.

- **Printing** information.

You can navigate around the Help area by following the instructions at the bottom of the screen - (PGDN) (Page Down, for more), (PGUP) (Page Up, to review earlier screens) and the (END) key (to exit back to the main screen). These keys are found just to the left of the numeric keypad on your keyboard (You can also try using the (ESC) key to return to previous screens; by using (ESC), you can go all the way back to the first Help screen if you so wish).

Also, you will note at the bottom of the main screen that there are other features available through "function keys" - (F2) allows you to change the color selections for your screen (this is entirely a matter of personal taste - if you really want orange lettering on a blue background, please be my guest), (F3) brings up a screen where printer parameters can be changed, and (F10) allows you to exit the program and return to the DOS prompt (If you opened Personal Numerologist from within Windows - you can go all the way back to the Windows Program Manager by typing in "Exit" at the DOS prompt after exiting either Personal Numerologist or Intimacy).

Entering Name and Date Information into Personal Numerologist

To leave the Help file screen, select the (END) button, which will take you back to the first screen, and then enter "N" for "no" and select (RETURN) or (ENTER). This will move you on to the first personal information entry screen titled "Data Entry Mode" (Illustration 6G). Here you are asked to enter the *number* of names in the "Birth" or "Current" name. A "Current" name is what you usually use to identify yourself (Barry A. Schwartz, for example), while a "Birth" name is the name on your birth certificate (Bernard Aaron Schwartz).

In terms of "numbers of names", a first, middle, and last name entry would require three name fields (three is the program's default number). A first name, *middle initial,* and last name would also require three name fields. "Mary Kathryn Anne Jones" would be four names, while "Jane Jones" would be only two names. You have the option of entering in anywhere from one to four names.

After selecting the proper number of names, select either the (RETURN) or (ENTER) key to bring up the first entry field and begin typing the first name of the person. After the first name is entered, select (RETURN) or (ENTER) again and the second and third fields, etcetera, will pop up in turn. Fill in the information as appropriate for your name, or the name you choose to enter. (Illustration 6H)

You may find that you'll want to rerun the program several times trying variations of the name used (for instance, with or without a middle initial, or using a nickname - such as "Bob" instead of "Robert," or vice versa). Numerology can

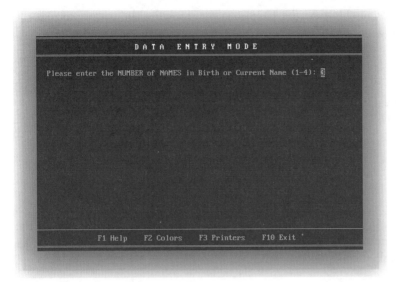

Illustration 6G. Enter the number of names in your "birth" or "current" name into the screen.

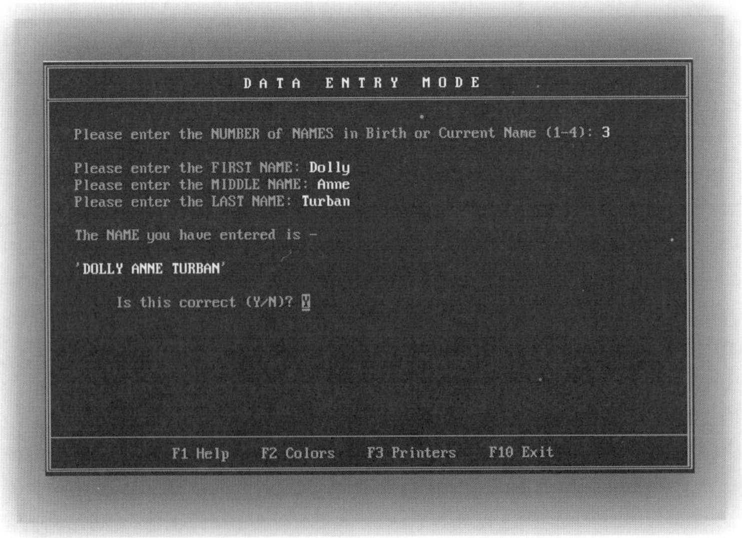

Illustration 6H. Enter your "birth" or "current" names into the name fields.

be used to choose a new name to help in one's career, to understand the character of a newborn baby, to see the effects of a woman's name change upon getting married or to name a business enterprise to achieve a desired purpose. Because of the different numerological "energies" present in the different name variations, you may find that changing the way you sign your name might bring about a change in luck for you. In fact, Dionne Warwick, the well known pop singer (and, as of late, a spokesperson for "Dial-A-Psychic" services), changed the spelling of her name at the height of her career in response to the advice of a numerologist. Using that middle initial that your mother insisted you use when you were a kid might not be such a bad idea after all!

After you enter the last of the names, you are presented with the fully entered name which you're then asked to verify. If you've entered the name correctly, go ahead and press the (RETURN) or (ENTER) key to get to the next screen; if incorrectly entered, enter "N" (for no) and then use the (ENTER) key to move to the incorrect field where you can then make changes. Use the (DELETE) key or the Spacebar to erase characters and then rekey the correct names.

The next screen (Illustration 6I) is where you will enter the birth date. Enter the month you were born (1 through 12), followed by the date (incorrect or "impossible" dates will result in a beep, although I did find February 31 is possible). Lastly, enter in the last two digits of "19__"; you can change the century

```
                    DATA  ENTRY  MODE

   Find the MONTH Number of the birth date from the following table:

              January    1        July        7
              February   2        August      8
              March      3        September   9
              April      4        October    10
              May        5        November   11
              June       6        December   12

   Please enter the MONTH Number of the Birth Date: 10
   Please enter the DAY of the Birth Date: 21
   Please enter the YEAR of the Birth Date: 1951

   The BIRTH DATE you have entered is 'OCTOBER 21, 1951'
        Is this correct (Y/N)? ▓


            F1 Help    F2 Colors    F3 Printers    F10 Exit
```

Illustration 6I. At this screen, enter the information for your birthdate, starting with the month, date, and then the year.

as well (for those persons born prior or after the twentieth century) by using the delete key to eliminate the "19" and substituting the century of choice.

Once the date is entered, the program will once again present you with the date in its full form for you to verify that the data is correct. If it's correct, press (ENTER) or (RETURN) to accept the data - if incorrect, key in "N" for "no" and use your (ENTER) key to navigate through the fields and change the information as necessary.

The next screen that appears asks you where you want the completed report to appear - your choices are either to view the report on your screen ("S"), or have it print out on your printer ("P," which is the default). If you'd like a print-out of the report, just select (ENTER) or (RETURN) and the report will be printed out on your printer (a second screen will appear to ask you if you prefer the printer to print out in a single sheet or continuous mode). If you want the report to appear on the screen first (you'll have another opportunity to print out the report at the end of the screen display), enter the letter "S" and hit (ENTER) or (RETURN) and the program will then come back within a few moments with the complete report on your screen.

Interpreting the Personal Numerologist Reports

Once you have selected your output (either Screen or Print) you will be presented with an extensive individualized report (around nine pages long) either about yourself or anyone whose data you've entered (See Illustration 6J for a sample screen from an actual report). These reports can reveal one's most intimate traits and desires, as well as giving new insights into friends and family. The reports also describe how to identify and take advantage of existing opportunities and how to open the way to new and even more favorable possibilities in your life.

The report contains many different commentaries, depending on what it discovers in the reduction and delineation process.

The following list of terms will give you some explanation for the interpretations of the personal numbers that are derived in Personal Numerologist. These definitions are excerpted from the Personal Numerologist manual that is available for you to print out.

 Life Path - The major lesson to be learned in life; where your opportunities for career and personal success are to be found.

Expression - Your special inborn abilities and talents, and how to make the best use of them.

Soul Urge - Your inner motivations and desires; what you really want from life.

 Birthday - Important personality characteristics.

 Master Numbers - Special energies indicating spiritual opportunities and the unique challenges they present.

● **Repeated Numbers** - Life energies that may be out of balance and how to harmonize them.

● **Karmic Debts** - Difficulties encountered until one learns how to use an energy that feels unfamiliar to one's nature.

● **Karmic Lessons** - Areas needing attention that, once mastered, can enhance one's life.

● **Modified Karmic Lessons** - Similar to Karmic Lessons but less intense.

● **Intensity Points** - Strengths or weaknesses in the personality because of too much or too little of a particular energy.

```
YOUR  STRONG  SPIRITUAL  AWARENESS  AND
ANALYTICAL    APPROACH   ---  AND   YOUR
INTROSPECTIVE,   DREAMY   SIDE


            YOUR 11 LIFE PATH AND 7 EXPRESSION

Your  strong  potential for spiritual awareness is  present  along
with  your other traits.   This energy is very special  and   isn't
available to most people.   Many, though,  who have this potential
aren't ever fully aware of it or,  in many cases,  become familiar
with  it  only when they're in their thirties  or  older.   If  you
choose  to  develop your spiritual side,  this energy may  play  a
vital role in your life.


When you use your spiritual awareness,  you probably   intuitively
perceive   a  great  deal  about  the  non-material  world  -- and
religious, psychic or metaphysical forces.  You have the potential
to  act  as a channel for these awarenesses.   You  can  learn  to

  Press END to exit, PGUP for previous screen or PGDN for more...
```

Illustration 6J. A screen from a sample Personal Numerologist Report.

To get the most value from Personal Numerologist, first run a report using the birth name (the same one that is on your birth certificate). Then run additional reports for any other names currently used or that have been used in the past. In numerology the birth name is the most important, but all names are significant.

Printing Out the Personal Numerologist Manual

To print out the Personal Numerologist manual from your hard disk, go to the Program Manager and pull down the "File" menu. Select "Run..." and enter the following command into your "Command Line" box:

```
C:  PRINT  PERSONAL\PNMANUAL.DOC
```

Then select "OK" with your mouse or, alternately, select (ENTER) or (RETURN) If you're going through the DOS prompt, simply type in the command-line command as above. This will provide you with a complete printed manual for the operation of Personal Numerologist, as well as some general information about the science of Numerology and information about how to register your program.

After you've printed out the report or have reviewed it on screen, you may exit the program by selecting the (F10) function key at the top of your keyboard. If you select (F10), the next screen that appears allows you to either exit Personal Numerologist or to start over and enter another person's name and birthdate, and generate another report.

When you exit the program, you will see information about registering the program and the added benefits that you will receive as a result, including telephone support, a book by Matthew Goodwin - *The Science of Numerology* - and credit towards upgrading Personal Numerologist to the professional version of the program, Numerologist Report Writer.

Checking Out Your Main Squeeze - Using "Intimacy" to See How Compatible You Are

Nowhere, probably, are people more vulnerable - or more curious - than when it comes to issues involving their personal relationships. Most people live out their lives in complete and utter confusion about their closest and most personal

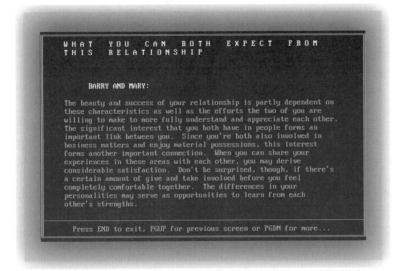

Illustration 6K. A sample screen from the report feature of
Intimacy.

relationships. It seems that - in spite of what's done or who does what to whom - relationships can develop bizarre lives of their own and turn overnight from 'kissy-kissy, huggy-huggy' situations into batches of sour grapes. Or, interestingly (and enigmatically) enough, sometimes just the opposite occurs! Go figure....

Divination techniques such as numerology have been consulted for ages to help provide insight into the powerful and rather fickle nature of Cupid's all-pervasive influence over the psyche of men and women.

With the Intimacy program, you now have an easy and fun way to personally access the insightful powers of numerology to help you better understand the labyrinths of your intimate relations. Using Intimacy, you enter data about yourself and your lover and obtain detailed reports which give information about the dynamics between the two of you, how you relate to each other, and how you can make your relationships better.

Intimacy is easy to use and very similar to the Personal Numerologist program, both in terms of its overall design and operation.

After you've copied the Intimacy directory to your hard disk (as discussed earlier in the chapter) you can then open the program and do a numerological comparison between two individuals. To start Intimacy, we use a very similar command string. Once again (as we did earlier with Personal Numerologist) if you're using Windows 3.1, go to the File Manager and pull down the "File" menu - then select "Run..." and enter the following into the command line:

```
C: INTIMACY\INT.EXE
```

then select (ENTER) or (RETURN).

Or follow the DOS and Windows 95 instruction for opening Personal Numerologist but substitute the Intimacy folder and files names.

The opening screen for Intimacy will come up in a DOS window and then you navigate through the data entry screens in a very similar manner as you did with Personal Numerologist. The main difference (in terms of entry) between the two programs is that Intimacy asks for *both* the "birth" names and your "current" names of the two people being compared. The difference, again, is that the "birth" name is the name as it appears on your birth certificate, whereas your "current" name is the name that you normally use in public, whether that name is a nickname (Jack instead of John; Susie instead of Susan, etc.) or perhaps an initial for a middle name. Or maybe the important issue about your current name is the *absence* of a middle name or initial altogether.

After you enter the data for both individuals, you have the option to either print out the report (the default is "P" for print) or to view the report on the screen (option "S").

Every report covers six important themes, each of which is divided into three sections—one for each of you as individuals, and one for the two of you as a couple.

The topics included in the Intimacy report include:

- **Your Adaptability**

- **Your Sociability**

- **Your Sensitivity To Your Own And Each Others' Feelings**

- **Your Ability to Give Love And Affection**

- **Your Ability To Earn A Living**

- **Your Mutual Ambitions**

As with Personal Numerologist, you can view the report as hardcopy (via your printer) or on the screen of your computer. When you are ready to exit, simply press (F10) function key, and you'll have to option to either exit the program entirely or to put together another report with either two other people...or maybe you and someone else ...or maybe a whole list of "someone elses"! (Pick a mate, any mate.)

Prime for the Macintosh

Okay you Mac folks, ready to look at some numbers? The numerology program that's included on the CD-ROM in the Macintosh area is a great shareware program called Prime (by Harold Feist of oTHERLOBE Software - Toronto, Canada).

Prime Info

The version of PRIME included in this book is a shareware demonstration version of the commercial program by oTHERLOBE. If you use and enjoy the demo, you are asked to upgrade to the commercial program. Please see the order page in the back of this book for ordering information.

You can run Prime from the CD-ROM, but you may find it easier or preferable to operate it locally from your hard disk (in particular if you want to store the files you create). To do this, simply open the *Digital Crystal Ball* CD-ROM icon (by double-clicking it), locate the "Prime Demo" folder and drag it over to your hard disk; this will create a copy of the folder and its contents on your hard disk. If you run Prime from the CD-ROM, you'll need to create a folder on your hard disk where you will store the files created.

Because the version of Prime included on the CD-ROM is shareware, there are a few features not available to you until you register and pay the shareware fees. For example, you cannot print out a file (but you can save an individual's name and birth data), nor can you save a report; you have to produce them "new" every time. You will be notified of features that are inaccessible to you as you navigate through Prime; don't worry - there aren't many.

Enough idle chit chat - let's get started! Like every Macintosh program, we open the program by double-clicking on the program icon (called "Prime Demo") which is found in the Prime Demo folder.

Remember what the essence of numerology is - numbers! You're not going to be confronted by groovy 3D animation or anything. In fact, what you'll first see (after you pass the intro screen where program and registration information is found) is a blank screen headed up with a menu across the top.

Go to the Open command under the File menu (or alternately select the ⌘-Ⓞ keys), which brings up the saved Prime data files for the individuals currently available to you. You'll be able to save your own files as well, but for now - let's look at an example that is already pre-saved for you. Search for and select the file for our intrepid online diviner, Dolly Turban. Do this by clicking on it with your mouse and then either select "OK" with your mouse, or simply press the (RETURN) or (ENTER) key. Prime will then calculate the numbers for Dolly and generate a report screen with information such as that shown in Illustration 6L.

Interestingly enough, a scrolling window name has been added at the top of the report window (which adds some visual interest to an otherwise rather meat-and-potatoes display). Should you choose to turn this scrolling feature off, it is a selectable feature under the "Edit" menu; simply select "Scroll Heading" to toggle this feature on or off.

As you scroll down Dolly's delineation (the numerology term used to describe a reading), you'll find the following components:

- **The personal numbers** (Birth, Destiny, Internal, Appearance and Survival). An in-depth explanation about the individual personal numbers as calculated for a particular person.

- **Alphanumeric Strengths and Weaknesses** - This explains what the frequency of certain letters mean in a name.

- **Personal Eras** - Here key emphases for periods in your life (birth through 31, 32 to 41, 42 to 51, 52 and afterwards) are discussed.

- **Personal Challenges** - These are the challenges and "karmic debt" to pay through each of the four Eras of your life.

Again, you cannot print reports from the shareware version of Prime, nor can you save reports you produce, but you can save files for names and birthdates for individuals - useful for quickly accessing an individual's report information, and an important feature when performing compatibility comparisons between two people (a feature we'll discuss later).

Macintosh Screen Print Secret

A good general purpose "trick" to know about the Macintosh is that you can save *any* Macintosh screen by holding down the key combination (SHIFT)-(⌘)-(3). A camera "shutter" sound is heard which is an indication that the Mac is saving anything (and everything) that is on the screen as a PICT file - creating a series of files named Picture 1, Picture 2, etc. These files can then be opened

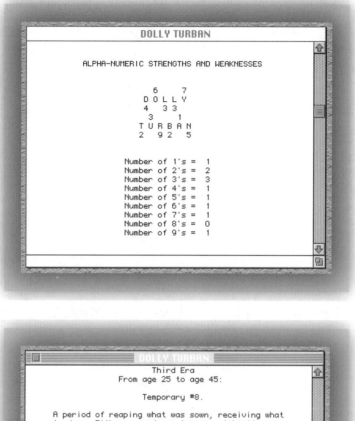

Illustration 6L. Some sample output screens from Prime showing the numerological delineation of our online diviner - Dolly Turban (for more screen displays, see Illustration 6O).

using any graphics application that can open the PICT file format (or the program Simple Text 1.2). From there, it *is* possible to get a printout. This is very cumbersome though, and is another reason to register programs like Prime to enable the print and save features.

Let's take a look at the menu selections within Prime, which will give us access to the intricacies of the program.

The menus are headed as shown - the **&**, **File**, **Edit**, **Personal Numbers**, **Applications**, and **Help**.

Under the **&** is an "About Prime" selection which gives info about the program's developer and about registering your program.

Under **File** are some of the standard Macintosh features - "Open," "Save," "Delete," "Print Setup," "Print," and "Quit." The "Delete" feature is included to delete Prime Name files if you so choose.

"Open" allows you to open any of the existing Prime data files. We'll be looking at the one for our "sample" - Dolly Turban - on our monitor. Again, as you work through this area, you will find that printing is not available in this version of Prime. Quitting Prime is simply a matter of choosing the "Quit" selection here on the File menu, or using the traditional ⌘-Q key commands.

Under the **Edit** menu are the standard "Undo," "Cut," "Copy," and "Paste" features, as well as the "Scroll Heading" toggle selection.

The **Personal Numbers** menu serves two functions. First, it allows you to quickly access (within a given reading) a particular section of a delineation without having to scroll through screens of data. You can quickly select

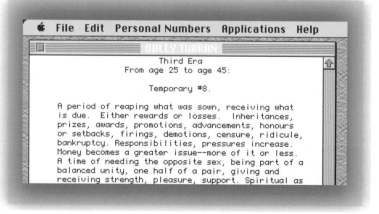

Illustration 6M. The menu headings of Prime - &, File, Edit, Personal Numbers, Applications, and Help.

172

Personal numbers, Alpha-Numerics (the strengths and weaknesses of the letters in your name), Eras, and the Challenges sections of a delineation .

And secondly, at the bottom of the Personal Numbers menu are selections which allow access to four additional subscreens: Personal Year, Personal Month, Personal Day, and Predictions. Entering data into these subscreens allows you to view numerological predictions for the active name on an annual, monthly, daily, or any future year basis.

Looking under the **Applications** menu selection we find "Mates and Partners...," "Choosing Names...," "Addresses...," "Review," and "Purge."

"Mates and Partners..." allows you to compare two individuals numerologically. You do this by selecting any two people for which entries and files already exist. Simply select the two people whose numbers you wish to compare - one at a time - by clicking on the file name. Prime will then bring up a report which compares their numbers and lets you see how they compare from a compatibility standpoint. This feature is limited not only to those celebrities already available to you, but to any files that you create for yourself, friends, lovers, enemies, etc.

"Choosing Names..." brings up a screen which allows you to check the numerological "quality" of a selection of potential names. This might be useful for those with a bambino on the way, or if you're just curious if you'd be luckier (or unluckier?) had your parents called you Maynard instead of Purcivel.

"Addresses" allows you to check out the numerological significance of the numbers in your address. (Don't bother entering the street *name* as it will be truncated to just numbers.)

The "Review" feature lets you recall a report (if you close its window down) and the "Purge" feature lets you keep things neat by clearing old reports from the screen before producing new ones.

Remember, should you ever have a problem or make a mistake with a file originally copied from the CD-ROM - you can always go back and recopy the original program or folder from the CD-ROM itself. Those files are permanent, unalterable, and always available to you.

The last menu, **Help**, is an extensive help system which can be accessed at any time, giving in-depth information about entering data into, and retrieving information from Prime, as well as some good information about numerology in general, and Prime's approach to the subject, in particular.

Entering Data into Prime

Let's look at what Prime has to say - numerologically speaking - about your name.

The first thing we need to do is select "Enter Data..." from under the Personal Numbers menu. Once selected, you'll see the entry screen, as shown in

```
┌─────────────────────────────────────────────────────┐
│ ▣ ▤▤▤▤▤▤▤▤ Enter Data ▤▤▤▤▤▤▤▤▤▤▤                      │
│                                                       │
│                    Subject's Name                     │
│            (as it appears on the Birth Certificate    │
│             or as it best identifies the subject.)    │
│         ┌───────────────────────────────────────┐     │
│         │            DOLLY TURBAN                │     │
│         └───────────────────────────────────────┘     │
│                                                       │
│      Year of Birth      Month         Day             │
│       (4 digits)       (1-12)        (1-31)           │
│        ┌──────┐        ┌───┐         ┌───┐            │
│        │ 1956 │        │ 8 │         │ 3 │            │
│        └──────┘        └───┘         └───┘            │
│                                                       │
│         Hour          Minute       "A"m\"P"m          │
│        (1-12)         (0-59)                          │
│        ┌───┐          ┌────┐        ┌───┐            │
│        │ 9 │          │ 46 │        │ P │            │
│        └───┘          └────┘        └───┘            │
│                                                       │
│   ┌──────────┐     ┌──────────────┐   ┌──────────┐   │
│   │  Cancel  │     │  P R I M E™  │   │    OK    │   │
│   └──────────┘     └──────────────┘   └──────────┘   │
└─────────────────────────────────────────────────────┘
```

Illustration 6N. The Prime entry screen with blanks for name and birth information.

Illustration 6N (titled "Enter Data"), appear. This is where you will enter name and birth information about yourself or whoever you choose; note that the top box is highlighted; anytime that you see the highlight, this means that box is ready to receive the information which you enter.

Type in your name. If there is another name showing, it will be replaced by your name, or whoever's name you wish to do a delineation for.

Note that, at the top of the entry screen, it suggests you either use the name off the birth certificate, or as it "best identifies the subject." Using the full formal name versus an initial for a middle name (or a nickname - Bob instead of Robert, for example), gives - as you might imagine - a different reading.

What Name Should I Use?

Numerologists vary somewhat on their opinions as to which procedure is best, but certainly are in agreement that different "energies" will be found by trying different combinations of names and initials. You may find - after you read the delineation - that you might want to consider adding (or removing) an initial in your signature! As the old Roman adage says - *Nomen Est Omen* - The Name is Destiny.

To get to the next group of entry blocks (the birthdate) simply either click the mouse on the appropriate box - or hit the (TAB) key. You'll often find that the (TAB) key is a good navigation tool around computer forms or data entry screens, and is generally programmed in as such.

Tab through the remainder of the boxes, entering in the right numerical values for your entries - the birth year (enter all four digits), then the birth month, and finally the birth day. In the birth time areas, enter in the time in hours and minutes (if you know it) or enter in 12 PM. (I might mention that your birth time is an important value to have handy as it is also needed in developing Horoscopes/Natal Charts in the Astrology programs.)

Once you have the data filled in correctly, then select the "OK" button with your mouse. Selecting "OK" cues Prime to start calculating the numerological values associated with your name, birthdate, and birth time. (A quick aside...normally programs are designed to accept the selection of either the (RETURN) or (ENTER) key as a substitution for "OK", but for some reason, this capability was *not* programmed into Prime; you *must* select the "OK" button with your mouse to enter in the data for your delineation.)

A Look at Prime's Interpretations...

If we look at the numerology reports that Prime creates for our sample delineation (our friend, Dolly Turban), we can get an idea of the kinds of in-depth information that Prime will provide about the personality of individuals. Obviously, you can use your own or anybody's name - or variations thereof - in Prime. You might even find it's fun to try out some of the samples included; several celebrities' names are included with the program and you might find it interesting to see what numerology has to say about folks like Jack Nicholson, Princess Di, Mick Jagger, Meg Ryan, even everybody's favorite highly over-exposed murder trial defendant - the O.J. himself (Hmmm, do you think maybe Judge Ito could have used Prime?). These and others are in the folder called "Celebrities."

Go to the Open command under the File menu (or alternately, select the ⌘-Ⓞ keys), and open the "Celebrities" folder which brings up the saved Prime data files for the individuals available to you, and select the file for Dolly Turban (if you haven't done so already). Prime will then generate and display the report information on the screen for Dolly, as shown in Illustration 6O.

Basically, you can use the Personal Numbers menu to quickly access the areas of the report that have the most interest to you. Selecting "Personal Numbers," "Alpha-Numerics," "Eras," or "Challenges" on the menu quickly accesses the part of the report that specifically deals with that area of Dolly's life. Alternately, you can simply scroll down the entire report and see each area in turn.

Now, select "Personal Numbers" from under the Personal Numbers menu. Prime will give you the screen display as shown here (Illustration 6O), which are the personal numbers as delineated for Dolly. By scrolling further down the screen you will get more detailed information about what each of Dolly's personal numbers means.

Choosing the other menu selections gives you different insights into all aspects of Dolly's personality. Dolly's delineation says she's versatile, fearless - even indifferent to danger, enthusiastic, and a good judge of character. On the flip side though, it says she needs to guard against an unstable temperament, infidelity ("jumping from job to job and love to love"), recklessness, and gambling. As you can tell - Prime is no wall flower when it comes to telling you about all aspects of your personality - both the positive and the negative. As such, Prime can make aware of your own potential shortfalls and foibles.

With Dolly's name in the "active" position, you can choose any of the other remaining selections under Personal Numbers - Personal Year, Personal Month, or Personal Day - to get a numerological prediction for Dolly for any day or period in the future. The "Predictions" feature at the bottom of the Numbers menu is similar to the Personal Year or Months selection, but gives more in-depth information about influences, and also splits the year in question into four-month periods, with commentary about the highlights of each period.

But how does ole' Dolly stack up compatibility-wise? What's to learn about her love life? Well, let's see how she compares with Lance Lothario, her heart-throb in the accounting department at the tuna cannery where she works. Granted, some of the attraction might lie in the fact that he's the sole heir of the owner, but who knows? Maybe it's her destiny to hook up with a tuna magnate! Lance's birthday is August 2, 1953 and hers is August 3, 1956 - just three years and a day apart, so let's see what happens when we put them together.

Go to the Applications Menu and choose the "Mates and Partners..." selection. This will bring up the dialog selection box where you can then select individuals with files that are already saved. (To check compatibility of two people, a file must already exist for both individuals.)

Select Dolly's name with your mouse and then select "OK," or hit the (ENTER) or (RETURN) key (contrary to the Data screen, the (ENTER) and (RETURN) keys do work when selecting a file). The very same dialog box will immediately return for you on the screen, and you should then select Lance Lothario's name. Within a few seconds, Prime will generate a report screen to you which will give you a compatibility comparison of Dolly and Lance (Illustration 6P).

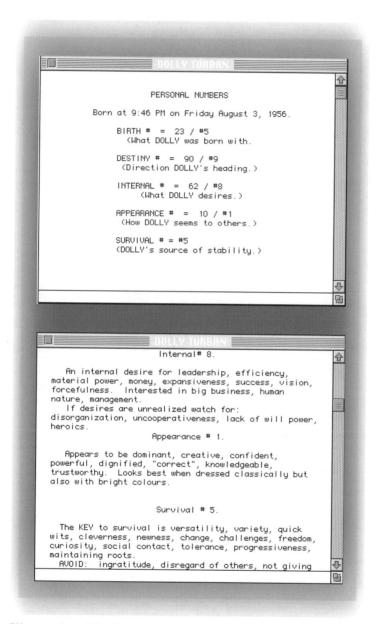

Illustration 60. On the top, the Personal Numbers for our friend, Dolly Turban; the bottom screen scrolls to show the details given by Prime to explain each of the personal numbers.

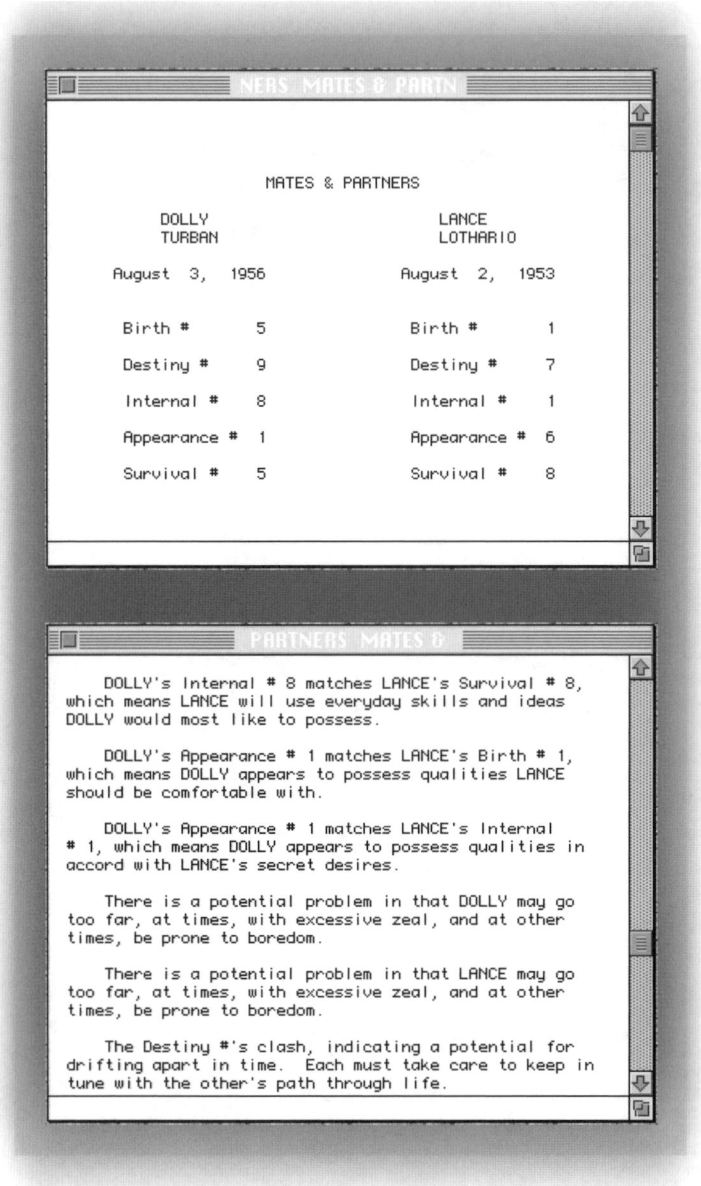
NERS MATES & PARTN
MATES & PARTNERS
DOLLY
TURBAN
LANCE
LOTHARIO
August 3, 1956
August 2, 1953
Birth # 5
Destiny # 9
Internal # 8
Appearance # 1
Survival # 5
Birth # 1
Destiny # 7
Internal # 1
Appearance # 6
Survival # 8
PARTNERS MATES &
DOLLY's Internal # 8 matches LANCE's Survival # 8, which means LANCE will use everyday skills and ideas DOLLY would most like to possess.
DOLLY's Appearance # 1 matches LANCE's Birth # 1, which means DOLLY appears to possess qualities LANCE should be comfortable with.
DOLLY's Appearance # 1 matches LANCE's Internal # 1, which means DOLLY appears to possess qualities in accord with LANCE's secret desires.
There is a potential problem in that DOLLY may go too far, at times, with excessive zeal, and at other times, be prone to boredom.
There is a potential problem in that LANCE may go too far, at times, with excessive zeal, and at other times, be prone to boredom.
The Destiny #'s clash, indicating a potential for drifting apart in time. Each must take care to keep in tune with the other's path through life.

Illustration 6P. To view the numerological compatibility of two individuals, choose the "Mates and Partners..." selection under the Applications menu. Select the files for both "partners" and a comparison will be performed, producing charts such as those shown above.

So what does their comparison say? Specifically, it says Dolly's Internal number matches Lance's Survival number (both #8's) and that "Lance will use everyday skills and ideas that Dolly would like to possess." What those skills might be is anybody's guess...tuna juggling? Balancing a checkbook? The ability to successfully hook onto the Internet?

Prime also says that Dolly's appearance number and Lance's Internal numbers (both #1's) match up and that "Dolly appears to possess qualities in accord with Lance's secret desires." To be perfectly honest, I'm not sure what Lance's secret desires are, and in the interest of not offending any of you sensitive-types out there, I'll refrain from speculation. I mean, really...who knows what odd thoughts might run through the mind of an accountant in a tuna cannery in a day?

But, then again, maybe Dolly's and Lance's odd thoughts mesh? Maybe life married to a tuna cannery tycoon is indeed a possibility for Dolly? At least the numbers seem to indicate so.

But finally, Prime suggests that Dolly and Lance's destiny numbers (#9 and #7, respectively) clash, indicating a "potential for drifting apart in time." I'm not sure about the numerological implications, but personally I'd suggest Lance better have some pretty good-looking tuna cannery stock options in his portfolio if he's planning on holding Dolly's interests for the long haul.

So - Dolly's destiny aside - I think you can see that generating a compatibility chart is a fairly easy thing to do. But remember, you can *only* perform compatibility checks on files that have been pre-saved. To perform compatibility checks for yourself and others, you will need to save to a file the name and birth information you entered under the Personal Numbers menu ("Enter Data..." selection).

Again, the last menu - Help - provides you with extensive assistance when entering data into Prime and/or when reading the interpretations. It is set up with the top six selections providing you general information about Prime (and navigating around in it), as well as a brief history and explanation of the science of numerology; even an explanation of how to handle leap years is included. The remaining four selections on the menu discuss (hierarchically) each of the menu sections' capabilities, and specifically how to enter and edit personal information.

The final selection at the bottom of the Help menu is "Suggestions." Suggestions gives you help on reading the various interpretations that Prime gives in the Personal Numbers area, and other advice as well, such as aligning yourself with individuals whose Alpha-Numerics compliment your own numbers to compensate for each other's shortcomings.

A final comment on Prime before we close out the numerology section. Remember that it is shareware...not freeware. If you find Prime or any of the shareware programs on the *Digital Crystal Ball* CD-ROM useful to you personally, then register and pay your shareware fees. Not only do you get a full-featured program with support from the author, but you also reap the resultant psychic rewards of an individual who is wise enough to know that there are no "free lunches" in the universe.

Like it or not, it all goes on your karmic credit card at the end of the month. And we all know that we have to pay off the cosmic Master Card - somewhere down the line.

PART THREE

A Journey of a Thousand Miles... Other Online (and Offline) Resources

Dark, except for the intertwined light and shadows cast by the fire burning low in front of him, the prehistoric shaman - clad only in a few tattered animal skins - crouches on the earthen floor of the cave, staring intently into the fire's dying embers. ☯ He traces the tendrils of smoke with his eyes, searching for a sign from the spirit guides - something to show him the location of the game so important to the survival of his tribe....

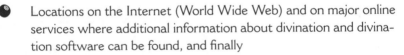

A priestess stares into a pool of water reflecting the clouds passing by over-head. Her eyes seek desperately to discern, in the ever-changing pattern, the outcome of tomorrow morning's battle with the nation across the narrow Mediterranean gulf, and the fate of both her people, and that of her handsome warrior son...

Under the cover of darkness, a slight seventeen year-old Austrian girl cau-tiously sneaks to the border of the village clutching a few precious coins. Ignoring the warning of the village priest, she seeks a Tarot reading by the Gypsy fortune teller camped in the meadow clearing. With a prayer of forgive-ness on her lips, she enters the dimly lit wagon to seek the fate of her lover - a soldier, silent for months now - conscripted to fight in a border war raging hun-dreds of miles away...

From the prehistoric shaman, to the oracles of the ancient Mediterranean, to the Gypsy fortune tellers of Eastern Europe - people the world over have always sought ways to answer the gnawing, perplexing questions concerning their lives. Although the methods have varied over time and cultures, they have often involved some sort of divination process.

Today, we have new tools for seeking information about the confounding questions of our future. The shaman, priestesses, and card readers of yore are rapidly being supplanted by specialized divination software (such as that found accompanying this book), and today, as we layout the framework of the Information Superhighway, we can even seek answers to our questions on the encyclopedic global information network known commonly as the "Internet."

In this last section of the book, we'll look at:

- A complete listing of the software included on the CD-ROM,

- A list of companies that produce and distribute divination software,

- Locations on the Internet (World Wide Web) and on major online services where additional information about divination and divina-tion software can be found, and finally

- A list of excellent reference books on divination and related topics that can be purchased at your local bookstore, or checked out at your local library.

182

A

Appendix A
Software Included
on the CD-ROM

The Digital Crystal Ball CD-ROM contains all the divination software discussed in this book. Both IBM and Macintosh programs are included on the same CD-ROM and can be accessed by a CD-ROM drive on either platform. It is recommended that you review the information presented in Chapter 2 (Your Journey Begins: Boot Up Your Computer and See the Light) which discusses general system requirements for both Macintosh and IBMs and compatibles, as well as discussing CD-ROMs and troubleshooting, should you run into problems.

There is a "readme" file (DCBINFO.TXT for the IBM and "Read Me First!" for the Macintosh) included on the CD-ROM which you should read first, immediately after you open the CD-ROM. Any additions, changes, deletions, errors, or variances from the book will be addressed in this 'readme' file.

In the book, we have provided similar programs for both the IBM and Macintosh platforms. The CD-ROM has programs for Astrology, Tarot, I Ching and Numerology laid out in a directory format as shown below.

Directory of CD-ROM

(IBM and Compatibles)

DCBALL (Top level Directory contains all the *Digital Crystal Ball* directories and associated programs and the 'readme' file.)

>**DCBINFO.TXT** (Text 'readme' file that describes changes, errata, additions to the CD-ROM.)

>**ASTROLGY** (Directory contains Astrology programs.)

>>**ASTRO** - Directory contains the "ASTRO for Windows" astrology program and associated files.

>**TAROT** (Directory contains Tarot programs.)

>>**VTAROT** - Directory contains the "Virtual Tarot Demo" Tarot program and associated files.

>>**CCROSS** - Directory contains the "Celtic Cross" Tarot program and associated files.

>**ICHING** (Directory contains I Ching programs.)

>>**SYNC** - Directory contains the "Synchronicity" I Ching program and associated files.

>>**DTRACK** - Directory contains the "Decision Track" I Ching program and associated files.

>**NUMRLOGY** (Directory contains Numerology programs.)

> **INTIMACY** - Directory contains the "Intimacy" numerology program and associated files.

> **PERSNUM** - Directory contains the "Personal Numerologist" numerology program and associated files.

> **GOODIES** (Directory contains two extra programs, Magic 8 Ball and Astro Ephemeris.

Macintosh

DIGITAL CRYSTAL BALL (Top level Directory contains all the *Digital Crystal Ball* directories and associated programs and the "readme" file.)

> **READ ME FIRST!** (Text "readme" file that describes changes, errata, additions to the CD-ROM.)

> **ASTROLOGY** (Folder contains the Astrology program for Macintosh.)

> > **VISIONS DEMO** - Folder contains the "Visions Demo " astrology program and associated files.

> **TAROT** (Folder contains the Tarot programs for Macintosh.)

> > **VIRTUAL TAROT DEMO** - Folder with the "Virtual Tarot Demo" and associated files.

> > **CELTIC CROSS** - Folder with the "Celtic Cross" Tarot program and associated files.

> **I CHING** (Folder contains the I Ching programs for Macintosh.)

> > **SYNCHRONICITY** - Folder with the "Synchronicity" I Ching program and associated files.

> > **I CHING CONNEXION** - Folder with the "I Ching Connexion" and associated files.

NUMEROLOGY (Folder contains the numerology program for Macintosh.)

PRIME DEMO - Folder that contains the "Prime Demo" numerology program and associated files.

GOODIES (Folder contains four extra divination programs, utilities, etc., including a Fortune Telling program, and a Tarot hypercard stack.)

In general, it is safe to assume that you will be able to operate any and all of the programs on the CD-ROM on your given platform (i.e., Macintosh or IBM), provided that you meet the following recommended minimum system requirements.

What's In Goodies?

Whether you're a Macintosh or IBM-compatible user, you'll find some interesting programs in the Goodies directory or folder on the CD-ROM.

IBM: 8-Ball for Windows - This little program is a tongue-in-cheek version of the old "Magic Eight Ball" novelty. Ask a question and get a response; you can even adjust the "optimism" of the readings. This light-hearted freeware is by David Lartique of Urbana, Illinois.

AstroEphemeris - A fully-functioning demonstration version of a Windows Astrology ephemeris generator by Ed Perrone, a frequent contributor to the GEnie Astrology Roundtable. This program is shareware. You are granted a license to evaluate the program on a trial basis for 30 days to determine if it meets your needs. If you continue to use the program after that time, you are required by law to pay the $29 registration fee. No cost of this book/CD-ROM collection is paid to the author of the program.

Macintosh: MacPredictions 1.0.1- A just for fun (we'll let you be the judge) "crystal ball" oracle; even helps you choose lotto numbers! This shareware is written by Neil Schulman of Oak Ridge Tennessee.

Tarot Reader 3.1.1 - A Hypercard stack put together to help you do four different Tarot card readings; profits go to the Gay Men's Health Clinic. Note that you will need the HyperCard application to run this stack. This shareware is by Anthony Vazquez of Brooklyn, New York.

Rosarium 2.0 - An daily oracle (with animation and sound effects) loosely based on an alchemical treatise from the 16th century called the *Rosarium Philosophorum*. This shareware was written by Rustle Laidman of Los Angeles.

Fortune Teller - A nicely designed application that uses captivating animation and sound to give you a crystal ball reading. This shareware was created by Gregory Katsoulis of Melrose, Mass.

Most of the bonus programs for the Mac are shareware, like AstroEphemeris for the PC. If you like them and want to continue using them, we urge you to register the programs with their authors. Each program provides registration details.

System Requirements

IBM-PC and Compatibles

 386 processor or higher (note: some programs will run on a 286 as well),

 DOS and Windows 3.1 or Windows 95,

 VGA monitor (256 colors) minimum,

 Sound Blaster card or equivalent recommended (for some programs),

 CD-ROM Drive,

 CD-ROM Driver software

Macintosh

 Mac LC or higher,

 5 megabytes of application (RAM) memory,

 CD-ROM drive (single speed supported but double speed is recommended,)

● Color capability recommended: 13" monitor capable of displaying 256 colors,

● Sound - built in or external speakers,

● System 7.0.1 or above recommended - Quicktime is necessary to play any video segments (version 1.6 or higher),

● CD-ROM driver software (if cache capable, it is suggested that approximately three Megabytes be allocated for smooth access to the CD-ROM),

(Note: Many of the programs included will run on a simple MacPlus, SE, or SE/30 running system 6.05 or higher, but the configuration as described is recommended to view all the programs.)

Appendix B
The World Beyond:
The Internet and Other
Online Resources

Other Divination Software Sources

The following companies are resources for, or producers of, software for divination. Some of the companies have contributed software that is included on the CD-ROM included with this book, and are so noted. Other software sources mentioned have been gathered from other sources, such as professional astrologers and psychics who use software daily in their practices, or from magazines and distributors specializing in metaphysical subjects, astrology, etc. This information is provided strictly as a resource and is not intended to be complete nor represent an endorsement of the products sold or developed by the companies listed, either by the publisher or the author.

Like any kind of software, there are good and "not so good" divination software packages. We suggest that, before you purchase any software, whether it is an I Ching program, a Tarot CD-ROM, or a word processing program - you check it out ahead of time. If possible, get a demo of it and read reviews from magazines, if available. Better still, seek endorsements from actual users of the products. Assure that the programs do what you want and need them to do before plopping down your hard-earned dollars.

A.I.R. Software
115 Caya Avenue
West Hartford, CT 06110
1-800-659-1AIR

Publishers of a full line of Astrology programs for amateurs and professionals alike. Headed by Alphee Lavoie, a professional astrologer with 30+ years of experience, AIR offers a full line of astrology related programs and products; IBM platform only.

Cosmic Patterns
P.O. Box 140790
Gainesville, FL 32614
1-800-779-2559

Publishers of the Kepler astrology package which is oriented to the professional astrologer. Numerous interpretation options are available. Some numerology programs are available, as well. Cosmic Patterns supports the IBM platform.

Lifestyle Software Group
63 Orange St.
St. Augustine, Florida 32084
1-800-289-1157

Publishers of Visions for the Macintosh (demo included on the CD-ROM) as well as another astrology program - Astroscopes. They also publish a Tarot program called Multimedia Tarot. Both IBM and Macintosh platforms are supported.

Matrix Software
315 Marion Avenue
Big Rapids, MI 49307
1-800-PLANETS

Matrix distributes a very professional catalog and has produced professional level astrology programs for several years, and the company has a center dedicated to ongoing astrological research. Their latest offering is a full astrology package called Win*Star for IBM Windows.

Synchronicity Software
2641 S.W. Huber St.
Portland, Oregon 97219
fax: 503-244-7749
Internet: paulo @ teleport.com
Publishers of Synchronicity, the I Ching program for the Macintosh and IBM and compatibles; demos are included on the CD-ROM.

Time Cycles Research
375 Willets Ave.
Waterford CT. 06385
1-800-827-2240
Software for Astrology professionals and students. Chart Interpreters, Atlases, Star Clocks, etc. Both Macintosh and IBM software are available.

Universal Software
P.O. Box 3683
Lakewood, CA 90711-3683
301-866-1274
A complete offering of shareware "metaphysical software" available exclusively for the IBM platform. Many good titles and a catalog is available on disk.

Widening Horizons
21713 N.E. 141st St.
Woodinville, Washington 98072
206-896-9810
Publishers of Personal Numerologist and Intimacy for IBM and compatibles; shareware versions included on the CD-ROM. Widening Horizons specializes in numerology applications which are widely used by professional numerologists.

Zephyr Services
1900 Murray Ave.
Pittsburgh, PA 15217
800-533-6666
Publishes a very colorful catalog of IBM software which covers numerous topics, with a heavy emphasis on astronomy. There is a complete "New Age"

software section that includes Tarot, I Ching, numerology, astrology, rune and graphology programs - just to mention a few.

Online Services

Those of you with access to any of the larger online information services (America Online, GEnie, CompuServe, e-World, Delphi, etc.) will find that there are areas and special interest groups available in each which discuss any or all of the divination techniques discussed in this book, and a whole lot more topics of interest in the area of Metaphysics.

Most of the services have areas set aside for hobbies and special interests such as divination where you can download software (many of the programs on this CD-ROM and similar ones are available from online services such as AOL and GEnie), read 'postings' (general questions or comments posted by interested parties and/or curious types) and even talk - online - to other interested parties, across the country or around the world, who have an interest in divination.

We will look briefly at the offerings of AOL, Genie, and CompuServe.

America Online (AOL)

Like most of its counterparts, AOL has developed an elaborate menuing systems for navigating through and accessing the 'meat' of the service, but it also offers the use of "Keywords" to navigate around as well. While you can get to areas of interest by using the menus, you can call up a Keyword at anytime (from any location) by using the (CTRL)-(K) key combination on the IBM, or the (⌘)-(K) key combination on the Macintosh. When the Keyword window pops up, simply type in the keyword and press (RETURN) (or (ENTER)).

Almost nightly, there are 'rooms' set up in the AOL People Connection area (the "chat" rooms) where Tarot card and psychic readings are performed; feel free to join in and have one of the readers read the Tarot for you, or have a psychic provide guidance and answers.

Also, there is an extensive Tarot section accessible in the Religion and Ethics Forum. First, use the Keyword ETHICS to reach the Religions and Ethics Forum. From the main Forum screen you will be selecting icons and folders that will contain the specific items and areas of interest (see more info in the outline diagram below).

With over 60,000 files available for downloading, it should come of no surprise that AOL has downloadable files (programs, text files, graphics, utilities, etc.) available specifically for those interested in divination and other metaphysical topics. Check out the Religion and Ethics Forum and the Crystal Ball Forum for details (see outline diagrams below).

AOL contains information about other metaphysical topics as well (including Numerology, Astrology, and Psychic Phenomena) accessible through the Hobbies and Interests Forum. Use Keyword EXCHANGE to reach the Hobbies and Interests Forum. See the Forum outline diagrams below for more information.

RELIGION AND ETHICS FORUM (Keyword: ETHICS)

    Message Boards (selection)

    List Categories (icon)

        New Age (category)

            Astrology Redux (folder with Astrology discussion)

        Pagan and Magickal Traditions (category)

            The Golden Dawn (folder pertaining to Golden Dawn Tarot)

            Crowley (folder with topics pertaining to Thoth Tarot)

        Religion Library Center (each of the following areas contains items related to astrology, Tarot, numerology and other divinational methods):

            New Age Library

            Pagan Library

            Philosophy/Metaphysics Library

            Applications Library

HOBBIES AND INTERESTS FORUM (Keyword: EXCHANGE)

    General Special Interests (category)

        Numerology (folder for numerology discussion)

        Psychic (folder for discussion of a general psychic nature)

        Astrology (folder for discussion of astrology)

CRYSTAL BALL FORUM (Keyword: CRYSTAL BALL)

Tarot Annex (Software/Books - has divination software for Tarot,
I Ching, numerology, etc. as well as associated texts and graphics)

Interactive Tarot (Nightly Tarot readings, 9 PM to Midnight EST)

GEnie

The General Electric Network for Information Exchange, or GEnie, is another major online service which has extensive files and special interest areas set aside for divination, metaphysics, and assorted "New Age" interests. In fact, the largest single area GEnie has set aside for this topic is the New Age Roundtable (at GEnie, each of the major areas is called a Roundtable).

Navigation around GEnie is different than AOL, but very straight-forward. After you have logged onto GEnie, you are at the top menu (page 1). From there, you will go to the Entertainment Services area (page 502) to select either the New Age Roundtable (page 1122), or the Astrology Roundtable (page 1180). Or, to get to the Religion and Philosophy Roundtable (page 390), first get to Symposiums on Global Issues (page 528) from the top menu. You will find navigational selections at each of these three main Roundtables to get to the other two quickly.

Within the New Age Roundtable, you will find real-time conferences with scheduled guest speakers and also an extensive software library where divination programs, Tarot deck graphics, I Ching programs, numerology programs and the like can be found. The following outline diagram represents GEnie's menuing structure and delineates the contents of the New Age, Astrology, and Religion and Philosophies Roundtables as well as the Astrological Forecasts Online Area; the page numbers listed are the page numbers of the main Roundtables.

Top (page 1)

Entertainment Services (page 502)

New Age Roundtable (page 1122)

New Age Bulletin Board

New Age Real-Time Conference

New Age Software Libraries

Astrology Roundtable (page 1180)

Appendix B
The World Beyond: The Internet and Other Online Resources

CompuServe

The final major online service that we will look at is CompuServe. Using the CompuServe Information Manager (the graphical user interface for either Windows or the Macintosh) you can access the New Age Forums (there are two - A and B) of CompuServe to take a look at the offering of divination software, real-time conferencing with other like-minded individuals, and general postings and information about divination and metaphysical subjects. From the Main Menu, select Home/Leisure and then Special Interest Forums (see the outline diagram below) to get to the actual New Age, Religion, and Religious Issues Forums where you will find literally hundreds of software programs, graphics, and textual information files. You can also quickly get to the New Age Forum by using the command GO NEWAGE (you can also access some Astrology information with GO ASTROLOGY) when you select the "Go" icons that pop up on the CompuServe subscreens, or by using (CTRL)-(G) on the Windows version, or (⌘)-(G) on the Macintosh version of the Compuserve Information Manager.

Main Menu

Home/Leisure

Special Interest Forums

New Age Forums (GO NEWAGE)

New Age Forum A

New Age Forum B

Religion Forum

Religious Issues Forum

In the back of this book, you'll find an introductory offer from CompuServe, which includes free online time. Note that you may even find updates to programs included with this book in the New Age Forum B.

Internet Newsgroups

There are several other major online services besides those discussed that provide similar offerings in the divination/metaphysical/"New Age" category. These include Delphi, Prodigy, and the Microsoft Network, to mention a few. These services, as well as the ones just covered, offer or will soon be offering various levels of Internet access. As such, they will be likely be offering access to Internet "newsgroups."

Newsgroups are repositories of information submitted by various individuals and groups with a common interest or topic - for instance, divination or astrology. You can "subscribe" to these newsgroups and get on their lists for electronic distribution. Consult the individual services that you may be using for more information on the Usenet groups (the larger cyber entities that manage the newsgroups) they are able to access and the particulars of subscribing to specific newsgroups.

There are many newsgroups available, for every odd, esoteric or just plain strange thing you might imagine (how about *alt.techno-shamanism*?). Check out *alt.tarot* (ongoing net discussion of all aspects of Tarot) and *alt.divination* (ongoing net discussion of myriad methods of divination) for information posted on the Internet about these two subjects.

Divining the Internet on the World Wide Web

For those of you with WWW (World Wide Web) level access to the Internet, the following "websites" are good sources for software, services, and general information about topics presented in this book. There are even a few sites where you can get a Tarot reading or an I Ching casting.

The Internet is a constantly evolving beast - and it is huge. As such, the locations listed are just a fractional sample of what is actually out there. With a growth rate that's rising faster then the national debt, it's safe to say that this list is nowhere near being "definitive," but I've listed what I feel are stable sites (i.e., I think they'll be around for awhile).

If you haven't done so yet, you'll find that a lot of the fun of "netsurfing" is in the discovery process itself - following threads of ideas and related concepts using the hypertext words that link you to other locations on the Internet, that - in turn - link you to even *more* locations. Don't be afraid to experiment and branch out. Click on a few of the links. Go off on a wild tangent. Explore and expand you horizons. Let your hair down. Take control and "cruise the net" to your heart's content. Don't worry, you won't fall into a metaphysical black hole or anything - but you just might find some pretty amazing things. Just remember to stop and eat occasionally, okay?

To assist in your searches, you may want to use a Gopher, WAIS or other search mode to perform your own searches for phrases such as "Tarot," "I Ching," "Astrology," "Occult," "Divination," etc. To aid you in that effort, I've listed a couple of Internet locations which are good to do general searches, and some suggested search terms, as well.

I Ching

http://www.shore.net/~rdl/iching/IChing.html
A general I Ching site with branches to several related online I Ching sites.

http://cad.ucla.edu/repository/useful/iching.html
This is the I Ching server at UCLA. Selecting this site will allow you to receive an online I Ching casting with complete interpretations that is different every time.

http://www.talis.com/resonate/iching/
A website to download an I Ching package called Talis I Ching Software. This Windows-based program includes engaging graphics, sound, and video icons.

Tarot

http://www.io.com/~fuzzface/
Full set of JPEGs of the Rider Waite Tarot deck - claims to be the "official copyright holders."

http://www.iii.net/users/dtking/tarot.html
dt king's Tarot Resource Page; Several good cross-links to Tarot texts, graphics, and software.

http://mist.npl.washington.edu/cgif/tarot
Website with a full set of GIFs of the Tarot Deck.

http://manor.york.ac.uk/cgi-bin/cards.sh
A tongue-in-cheek view of the Tarot included just for fun.

http://sunsite.unc.edu/otis/synergy/arcana/cards.html
OTIS Arcana Project Card View. A collection of Tarot card designs collected from artists on the Internet; some very nice images are shown as well as a good overview of the Tarot itself.

Astrology

ftp.magitech.com/pub/astrology
Good source for Astrology software for both Macintosh and IBM platforms; lots of programs, tutorials, etc.

Appendix B
The World Beyond: The Internet and Other Online Resources

http://www.links.net/ASTRO/

The Underground Astrologer; Contains cross-references to various websites discussing astrology; also has references to astrology software.

http://www.deltanet.com/users/wcassidy/astroindex.html

Asian Astrology Page. Dedicated to all aspects of Asian divination; sponsored by Tibetan Medical and Astrological Institute of Dharamsala, India. Really nice graphics and tools available specializing in Asian astrology, Feng Shui, I Ching, etc.

Other/Search Locations

http://wheel.ucdavis.edu/~btcarrol/skeptic/dictcont.html

The Skeptic's Dictionary. A great source for information on all kinds of strange stuff. Actually, it's a reference intended to provide a 'rational' view of tons of phenomena from Astral Projection to Oracles to Yeti. A very nice place to browse. You'll even find out what scapulimancy (an obscure form of divination) is!

http://www.cs.colorado.edu/home/mcbryan/WWWW.html

World Wide Web Worm. This Internet location is a good place to go to do searches (using a fill-in-the-blank form) for any topic that is of interest to you. You can conduct searches on more than 3,000,000 locations on the Internet from the WWWW.

http://www.utexas.edu/search/

This location, managed by the University of Texas, is another good location to perform searches for infomation available on the Internet. In addition, there is an extensive explanation of the search processes used for locating resources on the Internet.

http://www.lib.umich.edu/chhome.html

The Clearinghouse for Subject-Oriented Internet Resource Guides. This Internet location, maintained by the University of Michigan's School of Information and Library Studies, is an excellent place to look up Internet resources on almost any subject imaginable. Newsgroups, FTP sites, and individuals or groups are listed on thousands of subjects in the Sciences, Humanities and Social Sciences.

Suggested Search words/terms for more info

Here is a short list of a few of terms that you might use to search the various online services and the Internet for software, websites, news articles, etc. relating to the topics discussed in this book or for other information on divination, metaphysics, etc.

Metaphysics	Arcana
New Age	Fortune
Esoteric	Magic
Tarot	Spirituality
Divination	Kabbalah
I Ching	Religion
Numerology	Mythology
Astrology	Synchronicity
Ephemeris	Golden Dawn
Occult	

LightSpeed Publishing's Website

Like everything on the World Wide Web, the links mentioned in this appendix may change.

LightSpeed's website features a Digital Crystal Ball home page where we constantly update links to other interesting sites as well as point you where to go to get the latest versions of the software on the CD. Check out LightSpeed's website at:

http://www.lsp.com/people/calamar

To go to Digital Crystal Ball's home page click on the title of the book.

Appendix C
Bibliography

The following books are just a few of the resources available on the market and in your local library about divination, metaphysics, spirituality, and similar "New Age" topics. Many of the books listed were used as reference material for the topics discussed in this book, but there are literally hundreds more available. Look for them under the general category headings of "New Age," "Spirituality," "Metaphysics," or "Occult."

Tarot

Tarot Made Easy, Garen, Nancy (Fireside/Simon and Schuster, 1989).

A Complete Guide to the Tarot, Gray, Eden (Bantam Books, 1970).

I Ching

The I Ching or Book of Changes, Wilhelm, Richard; trans. by Baynes, Carl (Princeton University Press, 1985).

The I Ching Workbook, Wing, R.L. (Doubleday & Co., Inc., 1979).

Synchronicity: The Bridge Between Matter and Mind, F. David Peat (Bantam New Age Books, 1988).

The Portable Dragon -The Western Man's Guide to the I Ching, R.G.H. Siu (The MIT Press, 1968).

Numerology

Numerology and the Divine Triangle, Javane, Faith and Bunker, D. (Para Research, 1979).

Numerology - The Romance in Your Name, Jordan, Juno (DeVorss & Co., 1988).

The Numerology Workbook, Line, Julia (Aquarian Press, 1990).

Astrology

Grant Textbook Series: Elementary Astrology, Grant, Earnest A. & Catherine T. (American Federation of Astrologers, 1988).

The Astrology Game, Dean, Malcolm (Beaufort Books, 1980).

The Compleat Astrologer, Parker, Derek and Julia (McGraw-Hill Book Company, 1971).

Astrology: The Evidence of Science, Seymour, Percy (Arkana: The Penguin Group, 1990).

Practical Astronomy With Your Calculator, Duffett-Smith, Peter (Press Syndicate of the University of Cambridge, 1979, 1981).

Astronomy With Your Personal Computer, Duffett-Smith, Peter (Press Syndicate of the University of Cambridge, 1985).

Manual of Computer Programming for Astrologers, Erlewine, Michael (American Federation of Astrologers, Inc., 1980).

Divination - General

Body, Mind & Spirit: A Dictionary of New Age Ideas, People and Terms, Campbell, Eilleen and Brennan, J.H., (Charles E. Tuttle Company, Inc., 1984).

Appendix C   Bibliography

The World Atlas of Divination, Matthews, John (Ed.), (Little Brown and Company, Inc. 1992).

The Spiritual Seeker's Guide: The Complete Source for Religions and Spiritual Groups of the World, Sadleir, Steven (Allwon Publishing Company, 1992).

The Seeker's Handbook: The Complete Guide to Spiritual Pathfinding, Lash, John (Harmony Books, 1990).

Visions and Prophecies, (Time-Life Books, 1988).

Check out both mainstream and metaphysical bookstores in your area for these references. Don't be afraid to ask for help and recommendations, especially in the metaphysical bookstores; often the sales people there are a wealth of information. Many times you'll find that these same people are professional astrologers, psychics, or personally practice one or multiple divination methods. Another place that you'll find excellent reference materials for sale is at "psychic fairs." Also, you'll often find that these locations are good places to acquire divination tools such as Tarot decks, I Ching coins, and even more esoteric tools such as pendulums, dowsing rods - or even crystal balls.

And, as personal computers become more and more prevalent, there is an increasing likelihood that you will find divination software at these locations as well, ready for you to purchase and use - to allow you to gaze into your own digital crystal ball.

Index

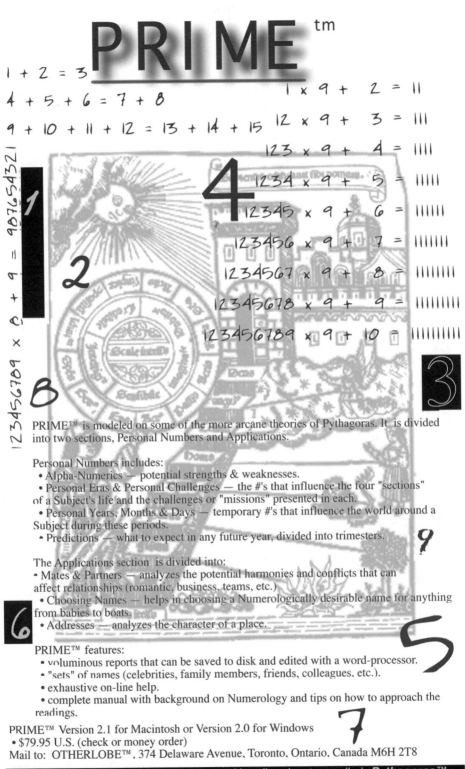

PRIME ™

$1 + 2 = 3$

$4 + 5 + 6 = 7 + 8$

$9 + 10 + 11 + 12 = 13 + 14 + 15$

$1 \times 9 + 2 = 11$

$12 \times 9 + 3 = 111$

$123 \times 9 + 4 = 1111$

$1234 \times 9 + 5 = 11111$

$12345 \times 9 + 6 = 111111$

$123456 \times 9 + 7 = 1111111$

$1234567 \times 9 + 8 = 11111111$

$12345678 \times 9 + 9 = 111111111$

$123456789 \times 9 + 10 = 1111111111$

$123456789 \times 8 + 9 = 987654321$

PRIME™ is modeled on some of the more arcane theories of Pythagoras. It is divided into two sections, Personal Numbers and Applications.

Personal Numbers includes:
- Alpha-Numerics — potential strengths & weaknesses.
- Personal Eras & Personal Challenges — the #'s that influence the four "sections" of a Subject's life and the challenges or "missions" presented in each.
- Personal Years, Months & Days — temporary #'s that influence the world around a Subject during these periods.
- Predictions — what to expect in any future year, divided into trimesters.

The Applications section is divided into:
- Mates & Partners — analyzes the potential harmonies and conflicts that can affect relationships (romantic, business, teams, etc.)
- Choosing Names — helps in choosing a Numerologically desirable name for anything from babies to boats.
- Addresses — analyzes the character of a place.

PRIME™ features:
- voluminous reports that can be saved to disk and edited with a word-processor.
- "sets" of names (celebrities, family members, friends, colleagues, etc.).
- exhaustive on-line help.
- complete manual with background on Numerology and tips on how to approach the readings.

PRIME™ Version 2.1 for Macintosh or Version 2.0 for Windows
- $79.95 U.S. (check or money order)
Mail to: OTHERLOBE™, 374 Delaware Avenue, Toronto, Ontario, Canada M6H 2T8

Watch for PRIME™ reborn soon as a multimedia adventure called **Pythagoras**™

Synchronicity (I Ching) Software Ordering Information

Synchronicity is an authentic version of the I Ching on floppy disks that runs on Macintosh and DOS computers. It has sold over 20,000 copies. Here is a small sample of unsolicited testimonials:

"Your program is a work of art and a piece of genius!" – L.Q., Milford, MA

"This program will transport you to other lands and times, even though you are sitting at a computer…Synchronicity is an excellent tool for familiarizing the user with the natural cycles of change and for revealing the ancient wisdom of the I Ching…for centering yourslef and reframing your perspective on a problem or issue." – Review in Whole Earth Review, Spring 91 issue

"Whoa! The answer to my first serious question was nearly identical to some recent legal advice which cost me $500!" – D.H., Vinton, VA

"Best new software: Synchronicity … works on several levels – as a game, a tool and a stress-buster … make better decisions … it represents a new direction … a breakthrough for personal computing." – The Seattle Times

"Synchronicity gives insight into, and takes the stress out of, making difficult decisions." – Success Magazine

"Synchronicity offers a unique way of breaking through creative barriers and accessing your intuition. Its responses are uncannily appropriate and almost always lead to a refreshing new insight into the issue at hand." – Review in PC Laptop Magazine

"Take a relaxing break without leaving your desk. Enjoyable and intriguing to use…providing useful answers…mood-altering, personal and friendly. I would recommend Synchronicity " – Review in MacWorld Magazine

Enjoy a lifetime of *Synchronicity* for only $49.95. Shipping/Handling is a total of $5.05 no matter how many units are ordered for delivery in the U.S. or Canada. (Shipping to other countries is $15.05.)

The unit(s) will be mailed to you, ***after receipt of your order and a check,*** and will include a disk set and manual for each unit. You will automatically become a registered user. The current version of Synchronicity will run on any Macintosh, PowerPC, or PC-DOS system. (If you are a Windows 3.1 user, you can still run Synchronicity under DOS.)

To order Synchronicity, please send a check to
Synchronicity Software 2641 SW Huber St.,Ste A, Portland OR 97219. You can fax Synchronicity at 503-244-7749, call 503-246-4043 or email paulo@teleport.com for further information.

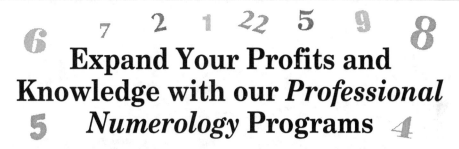

Expand Your Profits and Knowledge with our *Professional Numerology* Programs

Personal Numerologist and *Intimacy* are great programs to begin your exploration of the science of numerology. But if you require more in-depth reports or want to start a business selling reports for profit, you'll require the power of our professional programs. These programs allow you to start a business selling reports of the highest quality. You can set up your computer at Psychic Fairs, rent a mailing list or place a small ad and start earning income immediately. And if you do your own readings, there is even a program that does all the calculations for you.

Numerologist Report Writer

Produces fully integrated, *individual* personality reports with the same accuracy and clarity one would expect from a professional reading with a numerologist. These reports reveal the total sweep of a person's destiny with accurate and easy to understand text running 9 to 17 pages. For a total approach, the current name is compared to the original name at birth, showing new or increased potentials from the name change. $295.00

Yearly Report Writer

Produces in-depth reports that describe the important *yearly* and *monthly* influences that affect a person for the time period chosen. A one year report runs 11–16 pages and reveals the times of greatest opportunity as well as the times of potential difficulty. The likely events that will happen—as well as the preferred approach to those events—are described, showing how to get the most out of these experiences. $295.00

Relationship Report Writer

Provides a valuable way to explore *romantic* relationships. The highly insightful reports are full of practical suggestions that can help couples to have stronger, more meaningful partnerships. By showing the dynamics at work in the relationship, the reports can help two people to better understand each other and to improve their communications together. Reports run 14 to 18 pages and cover 12 important topics. $295.00

The Numerologist

Calculates and prints over 1065 important numbers for those who want to do their own interpretations. Includes the personality numbers, the points of intensification, the planes of expression, cycles, pinnacles, challenges and the complete progressions for every year from birth to age 91. $99.95

All report writers were developed by Matthew Goodwin, author of the definitive, *Numerology: The Complete Guide* and include the right to sell the printed reports in your regional area for profit.

Programs require an IBM PC or compatible with 320KB of RAM and DOS 2.1 or later. Both 3.5" and 5.25" disks are included.

Shipping and handling: $6.00 for 1–2 programs, $8.00 for 3–4 programs for U.S. and Canada. All other countries: $10.00 and $14.00 respectively. Payment must be in U.S. funds. Washington state residents, please add sales tax.